PUG

SMART OWNER'S GUIDE™

FROM THE EDITORS OF DOGFANCY. MAGAZINE

CONTENTS

Pug, a Smart Owner's Guide™
part of the Kennel Club Books® Interactive Series™
ISBN: 978-1-593787-62-2. ©2009

Kennel Club Books Inc., 40 Broad St., Freehold, NJ 07728. Printed in China.

*photographers include Tara Darling, Isabelle Français, Carol Ann Johnson,
and Karen Taylor; contributing writer: Juliette Cunliffe*

10 9 8 7 6 5 4 3

If you are considering a Pug to join your family, or have already succumbed to the Pug's many charms, congratulations. You are part of a wildly enthusiastic, worldwide group of dog lovers who refuse to consider the Pug a mere canine. Confidant, companion, cuddler extraordinaire–the Pug is all these things and more.

The American Kennel Club breed standard uses the Latin phrase *multum in parvo* to describe the Pug. That translates to a lot of dog in a small package. Truer words were never written. Even owners who don't typically consider themselves "small-dog people" happily make an exception when it comes to the Pug.

This is a dog with tremendous heart, personality, and appeal. Few Pug people can stop at just one. Perhaps it's a fawn and a black, or a male and a female. Something seems to compel lovers of the breed to share their lives with a pair of Pugs, or a peck of Pugs, or a pack of Pugs.

Live Pugs then give rise to the accompanying passion of collecting Pug stuff. From pillows to pins to prints to planters, there are

goodies out there in every medium to buy, sell, and trade.

Once adopted, Pugs get taken everywhere by their adoring owners. Although classified as a breed in the American Kennel Club's Toy Group, Pugs are big-boned and chunky. Still, they are wonderfully portable, and so you'll see Pugs with their owners riding the bus and the subway in major cities, as well as being transported by car and airplane. Many owners take their Pugs to work with them, and certainly most vacation in Pug-friendly destinations. The truth is: Pugs are just too much fun to leave at home.

The Pug is an equal-opportunity lover. This is one of the few toy breeds sturdy enough to make a good pet for kind, considerate children. No worries about bubble gum destroying a glamorous hairdo that trails to the ground. The Pug is a spit-and-polish breed, requiring just a weekly brushing, along with eye and ear cleaning and nail trimming.

Pugs are also exceptionally sociable. Introduced early to other pets in the household, Pugs are happy to hang out with the family cat, or dogs of other breeds no matter the size. No one told Pugs they were a small dog. No Napoleon issues here.

I won't go so far as to say that Pugs are for slugs, but exercise is not a chore with this breed. So if you're the kind of owner who drives by the local gym three times a week, a Pug will probably thrive in your household. A couple of short walks a day will suffice. If you live in a hot or humid climate, make sure those walks are taken in the early morning and the cool of the evening. No midday walks in the sizzling sun for this short-muzzled, flat-faced breed.

With this Smart Owner's Guide™, you are well on your way to getting your Pug diploma. But your Pug education doesn't end here.

JOIN OUR ONLINE Pug Club

You're invited to join **Club Pug**™ (**DogChannel.com/Club-Pug**), a FREE online site with lots of fun and instructive online features like:

◆ **forums, blogs,** and **profiles** where you can connect with other toy-dog owners

◆ **downloadable charts** and **checklists** to help you be a smart and loving Pug owner

◆ access to **e-cards, wallpapers,** and **screensavers**

◆ interactive **games**

◆ Pug-specific **quizzes**

The **Smart Owner's Guide**™ series and **Club Pug**™ are backed by the experts at DOG FANCY magazine and DogChannel.com—who have been providing trusted and up-to-date information about dogs and dog people for forty years. Log on and join the club today!

Is the Pug a comic, a clown, a portable companion welcomed everywhere, or a barometer of his loved ones' every mood? All of the above. Non-Pug owners consider him just a dog. That's where Pug people beg to differ.

Allan Reznik
Editor-at-Large, DOG FANCY

Pugs are possibly the luckiest dog breed on the planet. They have their own parties, they aren't expected to work, they can snore as loudly as they like and won't get relegated to the living room couch, and their owners love them with a loyalty and passion that's almost religious. Fortunately, the loyalty and love are reciprocal, and Pugs aren't shy about showing it.

For the "Pug Pious," the Pug isn't just a dog, but a person disguised as a Pug; and not just any type of person, but royalty. Most Pug households have more than one Pug in residence: kings and queens of Pugdom teach their humans how life should be lived, Pug style. Even smart owners are often out-witted, being the dumber of the two species, of course, and because they don't always follow the Pug Rules of Life, which include, "The Pug gets the best spot on the bed," and "The Pug shall have access to all contents of the refrigerator on demand."

Breed enthusiasts describe the Pug as "the perfect blend of dog appeal and wistfulness." A Pug will readily keep his owners amused

it's a Fact

In the 1997 movie *Men in Black*, a Remoolian alien took the form of Frank the Pug, played by a Pug named Mushu. Director Barry Sonnenfeld liked the little dog's performance so much that he expanded the part in the *MIB* sequel five years later.

Pugs are known for their huge and sparkly eyes, as well as their huge and lovable personas.

and entertained for hours on end with his clown-like personality. Ownership of Pugs often runs in human families, with several generations having happily owned the breed. This is a personality dog, one just as comfortable living in a small home as he is in a spacious one. Some Pug owners call their Pugs "little people," and when you know the breed, it's easy to understand why!

The Pug's bark is surprisingly deep for the breed's size. Indeed, a Pug is usually a good watchdog, ready to bark when the doorbell rings or when someone approaches the house. If you are a light sleeper, it's worth bearing in mind that although not all Pugs snore, many do!

An exceptionally clean little dog, the Pug is remarkably free from doggie odors. Some consider the Pug a suitable breed for seniors and the disabled, though you should not forget that Pugs, like all other dogs, require some exercise. All things considered, a Pug usually seems happy to be whatever his owners need. He can be content to roll up in a ball at your feet while you are knitting or watching TV, he will enjoy a lively ball game, or he can just be a friendly clown, providing entertainment for his audience at home.

Although the origin of the breed lies in China, the Pug dog differs considerably in his personality from many of the other breeds from the Far East in that he doesn't display the usual reserved air of superiority. The Pug is a unique breed in many ways and has numerous admirers, in part because of his puckish sense of humor and engaging ways.

PHYSICAL CHARACTERISTICS

Small, squarely built, and cobby, the Pug has well-knit proportions and a certain hardness of muscle, making him a strong little animal and quite different from the majority of breeds in the Toy Group. Ideal weight is 14 to 18 pounds, but certainly some are heavier, and there are probably few males weighing less than 18 pounds. Although the breed standard does not differentiate between the size of male and female Pugs, generally males are somewhat larger.

You should always remember that Pugs usually enjoy their food and might be considered rather greedy. Therefore, it is necessary to keep strict control of your Pug's diet so he doesn't become overweight. Once a Pug has reached the stage when he carries too much weight, it's extremely difficult to get the weight off!

A Pug's chest is wide, and the his body is set on strong legs. His large, round, wrinkled head with dark, globular eyes is offset at the rear by a high-set tail, curled tightly over the hip, with a double curl being highly desirable.

Did You Know?

The Pug's coat lies flat, but individual hairs can actually be 1 to $1\frac{1}{2}$ inches long. Many fawn Pug owners stop wearing black and navy, and black Pug owners stop wearing white, linen, or yellow because of the constant shedding.

COLORS AND COAT

Pugs come in silver, fawn, and black, although silvers are few and far between. Although not mentioned in the breed standard, fawn and silver Pugs have a double coat, which consists of an outer weather-resistant coat and a softer, insulating undercoat. Black Pugs have a single coat.

Colors are clearly defined and should have a black line extending from the back of the head along the top of the back to the twist of the tail, called a trace. The mask (or muzzle) should be as black as possible, as should the ears, moles on the cheeks, and the diamond or "thumb mark" on the dog's forehead.

Many breeders consider the overall quality of today's black Pugs to be inferior to Pugs of the past. However, there is still a handful of top-quality black specimens that are capable of holding their own with the best, comparing favorably with those of years gone by. Unfortunately, there are only a few breeders currently specializing in black Pugs. It's difficult to breed good black Pugs because the coat should be jet black with no other mark-

Pugs are prone to flea allergies, so keep your Pug fresh and clean on a daily basis.

ings visible. Because of the color, the desired wrinkles on the head need to be deep and clear in order to be seen.

Regardless of color, a Pug's coat is easy to maintain, for it is fine, smooth, and soft. This is a short, glossy coat that should be neither harsh to the touch nor woolly. Pugs' coats do shed to a certain extent, though not so much as those of many other breeds. People with sensitive allergies ought to check before buying a Pug that the coat does not affect them. Always keep in mind that a dog will remain with you for life, so you must be certain that you are making a well-informed decision before deciding upon a particular breed.

On the subject of allergies, some Pugs themselves suffer from flea allergies, so it is important to keep your Pug free from parasites.

Because of the wrinkling on a Pug's head, special care needs to be taken to keep this area clean to avoid any build-up of dirt and bacteria that can cause irritation to the skin.

THE TALE OF THE TAILS

The Pug's twisted tail is natural and is not cropped to look this way. In fact, the tail is not so short as you might think at first glance—it's just well-curled. It has recently been realized that a few Pugs suffer from a vertebral problem, apparently because of the curled tail. This is usually noticed before the age of twelve months and can cause a dog to be crippled.

Forehead wrinkles are a classic breed trait and should be regularly cleaned; now those are some wrinkles to love!

Pugs tend to have low energy, so keep your Puggy active and fit with plenty of exercise.

PUG PERSONALITY

This is a breed with great charm, dignity, and intelligence, though, like other intelligent breeds, he can be rather self-willed. The Pug is an even-tempered breed with a happy, lively disposition. The friendship displayed is often effusive; indeed, most Pugs seem constantly delighted to meet people and they show special affection toward children. However, although the Pug shows friendliness toward strangers, it is to his owner and family that he is most devoted.

The Pug is a fearless breed that, despite his diminutive size, enjoys exercise outdoors and has something of a brave, sporting instinct that can occasionally cause him to run into trouble with other dogs. That is not to say that Pugs are generally aggressive, though they might appear so sometimes because of jealousy.

Inside the home, the Pug likes nothing more than warmth and comfort, with general affection and petting bestowed on him by his owners.

Other endearing Pug traits include:

■ Pugs were bred to be pampered, and they seem to know it, but they also seem to know that pampering should be reciprocal.

NOTABLE & QUOTABLE

Exercises may include tug games, retrieving, swimming, accompanying owners when they walk, play dates with other dogs, or calling the dog to come or jump in the backyard over a series of low jumps.—trainer Beverly Hebert from Sugar Land, Texas

Among the herders and the guard dogs, the hunters and retrievers, the Pug may seem like the laziest member of Dogdom. However, it takes a long time to master the wide-eyed head tilt, the I-want-a-biscuit snortle, and the tushie-tucked boogie.

Pugs crave a lot of human companionship. This breed is very human-like in his

A fun mix of silly and smart, Pugs are adoring companion pets.

expressions and mannerisms. Some Pug zealots refer to their breed of choice as "fur people." Pugs tend to be sedentary and have earned the moniker, couch *pug*tatoes, because they dedicate a lot of time lolling around the house.

■ Though the Pug is a lap dog, he isn't a pushover. The Pug isn't the slowest salmon in the stream, either, no matter what the Pug dilettantes say.

■ Pugs can be quite impish and rarely take no for an answer, even if it's for their own good. They are ingenious when they want to be, and will often get themselves into trouble.

■ Pugs are loving, silly, intelligent beasts, but they can also be high maintenance pets and are best owned by someone willing to deal with their physical quirks. Pugs aren't

"hot-weather friendly," nor do they make the best jogging buddies.

■ Don't forget the shedding!

■ The Pug is more likely to train his owner than the other way around. Many people find Pugs difficult to train—OK, impossible to train. But maybe those people are just suckers for the big-eyed, tilt-headed manipulators.

■ Pugs can be stubborn.

■ New Pug people had better get used to attention, and fast. Possibly no other dog breed engenders the public response that the Pug does.

■ Pug novices, take note: Pugs snuffle, snort, and sneeze, and may keep you up at night. However, Pug enthusiasts are nothing short of charmed by their Pugs' snorting symphony.

PUGS AND CHILDREN

Pugs certainly seem happy in the company of children, and usually the feeling is mutual. This is a breed that always seems ready for a bit of "rough and tumble," but always supervise dogs and children. If taught to respect dogs, children can spend many happy hours in the company of a Pug. Nevertheless, adults should never allow either to become overexcited.

HEALTH CONSIDERATIONS

Because of the Pug's short foreface, the breed can suffer breathing difficulties and does not easily tolerate extreme heat. In general, though, the Pug is a reasonably

Pugs and children are like peanut butter and jelly: they know how to mix!

When Pugs are excited and running full force around the house or yard with their butts pointing downward, we call it 'Pugtona,' in reference to the Daytona 500 car race,"

—Lisa Sori, Pug owner from Las Vegas, Nev.

healthy breed and can live until a ripe old age. It is, however, worth bearing in mind that often Pugs do not take well to anesthesia, so it is important to mention this to your vet if an operation is pending.

Pugs, like other short-nosed (brachycephalic) breeds, can be prone to elongation of the soft palate. The Pug has been bred for centuries to have a short nose and wrinkled skin; as a result, the soft palate tends to be wide and flabby. As the dog pants, the soft palate gets drawn back into the larynx so that air is unable to enter the lungs. This causes Pugs to suffer distress in unusually hot weather or following exertion.

Keep a careful eye on your Pug in hot weather and always be on the lookout for any sign of fatigue during exercise. Danger signs are protruding, staring eyes, and holding the head high in an effort to draw in more air. A Pug can lose consciousness and his breathing may stop, but sometimes will resume within only a few seconds.

Any dog can suffer distress or even die if left in a car on a warm day, even with ventilation. Pugs are even more likely to be affected, so beware! Never leave your Pug alone in a car.

Should your dog suffer from heat exhaustion, cold water or ice should be put on his head, face, and body immediately; your dog should also be kept cool and quiet.

Here it is worth mentioning that food should never be given immediately before or following strenuous exercise. Opinions vary, but a good rule of thumb is to allow a full hour's rest before or after any meal.

A Pug's eyes should be globular in shape, but they should not be too bulbous. This shape can bring with it various problems because eyes are more likely to be exposed to injury or damage when dust becomes entrapped. Smart Pug owners ensure that there are no rose bushes with thorns or any other spiky plants in their gardens.

Pugs have lots of physical quirks, so extra care must be given to this breed.

Pugs are prone to eye and breathing problems. Owners must be especially cognizant of these potential problems and remove objects from their homes and yards, such as rose bushes and cacti, that might injure a Pug's sensitive eyes.

Take into account that Pugs are shedders before you decide if you want to allow him on your furniture.

The Long and Snort of It

Pugs aren't exactly quiet dogs. Here are what some owners say about the sounds their little dogs make.

"There is nothing quite like a quiet Sunday afternoon listening to the rhythmic snoring of a comfortable Pug!"
—*Julie A. Pizzolato, Pug breeder, Priest River, Idaho*

"They can snore louder than the band! Once, when my in-laws were spending the night, and not too long after Buster joined our menagerie of dogs, they awoke early one morning to very loud snoring. Each wondered if it was the other. Harry thought, 'Is that Edith?' Edith thought, 'Goodness, is that Harry snoring?' Over breakfast, we confirmed it was Buster sawing logs like a lumberjack!"
—*Mary Carolyn Stewart, member of Alabama Pug Rescue and Adoption, Meridian, Miss.*

"It is true that Pugs are snorting, snoring, snot-spitting babies, and unless you are absolutely in love with these little clowns, that description is not going to be appealing to everyone. Pug people live each and every day to be loved by a Pug, and no amount of snoring or snorting would be frowned upon. There are humorous moments when your Pug is sleeping next to you, and you're wide awake because your spouse is snoring, and your Pug starts up, too! Moments later your spouse will be riddled out of his sound sleep, saying, 'Get that dog out of here! He's snoring so loud I can't sleep!' If he only knew the truth."
—*Lisa Sori, Pug owner, Las Vegas, Nev.*

"I often think that at night, if an intruder were to break into my house, my Pugs would not be able to hear it over their own snoring. But once you get used to the sound, it seems eerily quiet without it. I can't fall asleep without the sound of little Pug snores in the bed."
—*Roxane Fritz, board member of Pugsavers, a rescue group in northern California*

Pugs provide tons
of comfort to their
owners; even their
snoring is soothing!

PUG PROFILE

This breed is a lot of dog in a small package!

COUNTRY OF ORIGIN: China

WHAT HIS FRIENDS CALL HIM: Mops, Carlin, Puggy

SIZE: 14 to 18 pounds

COAT & COLOR: fine, smooth, and short coat. The colors are fawn or black.

PERSONALITY TRAITS: affectionate, sociable, and loyal. Pugs were bred to be companion dogs, and they do their job well. They are playful, clever, and have a happy disposition.

WITH KIDS: these friendly dogs get along well with people of all ages

WITH OTHER PETS: good with other pets

ENERGY LEVEL: low

EXERCISE NEEDS: Pugs need daily walks, but they are sensitive to strenuous exercise and cold and hot weather because of their short noses, which make breathing difficult.

GROOMING NEEDS: require brushing at least twice a week. Pugs' facial wrinkles also need regular cleaning.

TRAINING NEEDS: These highly intelligent dogs are especially sensitive to tone of voice, which makes them easy to train and punishment unnecessary. They bore easily, so training practices should be varied.

LIVING ENVIRONMENT: Pugs are relatively inactive indoors and can live anywhere, provided the temperature is comfortable.

LIFESPAN: 12 to 15 years

IN TIME

Pug-type dogs have been keeping people company for centuries. Pug lore claims that the breed has been known for more than 2,400 years, but such claims are impossible to authenticate because breeding records have been kept for only the past 150 years or so. Nonetheless, dogs resembling Pugs are said to have been found in Tibetan monasteries and in Japan and China, long before the Christian era. The Pug's small size, curled tail, and flat face are certainly representative of the dogs favored in Asian cultures.

CHINA AND THE PUG

In China, there has long been a breed of dog known as the *Happa* (sometimes spelled Hapa), which is similar to a smooth-coated Pekingese. Indeed, many people believe that the *Happa* may be the progenitor of the Pug. Short-mouthed dogs in China are known as *Lo-sze*, and although they may well have been known there as far back as 1115 BC, there is no record of them until 663 BC. The *Lo-sze* had clear features distinguishing it from the Pekingese: the muzzle was differ-

Did You Know? A few times a year, depending on the local temperatures, your Pug will "blow coat," meaning he will shed more heavily than normal. Some Pugs have a double coat (a top coat and an undercoat), doubling your shedding possibilities. On the positive side, the Pug coat is so short and smooth that it doesn't build up or mat like other types of coats.

ent, the coat was short, and the ears were small and vine-shaped. By AD 732, there are records of a small, short-faced dog, known as the *Suchuan pai* dog, that was among gifts sent from Korea to Japan.

In China, dogs were frequently treated almost like royalty, even with titles of rank being bestowed upon some of them. They were carefully guarded, and many owners employed servants to care for the dogs and to see that they enjoyed every comfort. Understandably, the Pug was owned primarily by those within court circles or from the ruling classes of the country, and often the dogs were treated primarily as ornaments.

The Pug was popular in China at least until the 12th century, but then interest waned and little mention of the breed was made until early in the 16th century.

ON TO EUROPE

Pugs have been very popular in Holland, though in the early years, they were known as "Dutch Mastiffs." This name may help explain the confusion that arose over the breed's origin. Pugs from Holland were certainly destined to have a great influence on the spread of the breed throughout Europe.

The Dutch East India Company played an important role in trade with the Orient. On many of the ships' return journeys, both Pugs and Pekingese were brought back as precious cargo.

it's a
Fact

The American Kennel Club accepted Pugs for registration in 1885, making it one of the earliest recognized AKC breeds. The first Pug registered by the AKC was a dog named George.

Historians suggest that Pugs were introduced to Holland by the Portuguese, who opened sea routes for trading with China early in the 16th century. It's also suggested that Pugs came to Holland via Russia, then known as Muscovy. The aunt of Russia's Catherine the Great was reputed to have kept a score of Pugs and the same number of parrots in a single room. Perhaps equally fascinating is that several of this Princess's dogs always accompanied her to church.

Whatever the case, when enterprising European traders made their way to the Far East, they were no doubt captivated by the little dogs and brought them back as part of their cargo. They were secure with the knowledge that such an unusual animal would find favor in royal courts, where toy breeds led pampered lives as lap dogs, foot warmers, and flea catchers.

The Pug's roster of royal fans included Napoleon Bonaparte's empress, Josephine. Her dog, named Fortune, kept her company while she was imprisoned during the French Revolution. Fortune served as her courier, carrying messages to Napoleon, who wasn't always in Fortune's favor, however. The protective Pug is said to have bitten the future emperor when he entered Josephine's bedroom on their wedding night. That's not to say that Napoleon didn't secretly admire the breed. "I would rather have an army of dogs led by a Pug than an army of Pugs led by a dog," he is supposed to have said.

The Pug's popularity with royals and commoners continued into the 19th century. Queen Victoria, a noted dog lover, kept a number of breeds, including Pugs, in the royal kennels. When Britain's Kennel Club was formed in 1873, its first stud book listed sixty-six Pugs. The breed was especially promoted by Lady Willoughby d'Eresby and a Mr. Morrison of Walham Green.

Pugs became so well-liked that canine commentator Alex Dalziel said in 1870: "The Pug market is over-stocked and everywhere in town and country these animals swarm." That doesn't mean, however, that the dogs were of high quality. Two years later, Thomas Pierce, writing under the pseudonym Idstone, said: "It would be hard to find more than half a dozen specimens equal to what existed a hundred years ago."

The breed began to change during this time, in part because of the arrival of a fresh supply of Pugs from the Far East. After the second opium war between the English and French against Chinese in the late 1850s, returning officers brought more Pugs, including some black Pugs, which were a novelty. The black Pugs were first exhibited in an English dog show in 1886 (four years after the formation of the British Pug Dog Club). The Chinese Pugs helped bring about a change in the breed's looks, having shorter legs and more pushed-in faces than the Pugs that had been in Europe for the past three centuries.

THE PUG GOES TO ENGLAND

William of Orange, the grandson of William the Silent, went to England with his wife, Mary, in 1688 to take the throne. The couple brought with them Pugs, each wearing an orange ribbon around his neck to denote its connection to the Royal House of Orange. The breed quickly found favor in England, where it soon became known as the Dutch Pug, and later, Pug or Pug-dog.

Once upon a time, Pugs rubbed elbows with kings and queens!

In 18th-century Britain, the Pug became highly fashionable, not only at court but also among people of "quality." Indeed, when ladies ventured outdoors, it was quite "the done thing" for them to be accompanied by a turbaned servant and a Pug. Queen Charlotte, wife of King George III (1760–1820), was also inordinately fond of the breed and had many, one of which is depicted in a painting hanging in Hampton Court. However, by the end of the reign of George IV in 1830, the Pug was no longer fashionable and by the middle of the 19th century the breed's popularity had fallen.

The decline of the Pug was by no means averted by the author Taplin, who wrote of the Pug, "…applicable to no sport, appropriated to no useful purpose, susceptible of no predominant passion…" Such comments could surely not have served to enhance the popularity of the breed that all too quickly became known, rather contemptuously, as an "old lady's pet."

But the Pug did not remain out of favor for long, thanks in part to Queen Victoria, who was such an ardent dog lover and who owned Pugs among several other breeds. It is likely that her earliest Pugs were given to her by royal European relations. Her dogs appear to have been kept as nursery dogs, most appropriate for this breed that gets along so well with children.

The Prince of Wales gave a Pug named Bully to his wife, Queen Alexandra, before leaving for an Indian tour. Of course, Queen

During the 1800s, Pugs were a symbol of high fashion among the wealthy and elite.

Alexandra, too, was famous for her devotion to dogs and took an active interest in dog shows, an increasingly popular activity, particularly among Pug owners.

There were two main Pug strains in Britain in the early decades of the 19th century. A publican by the name of Mr. Morrison bred pale fawn Pugs in Waltham Green, and Lord and Lady Willoughby d'Eresby used imported blood to improve type. There is

SMART TIP!

Every day, you should clean your Pug's delicate facial folds with a soft, damp cloth or a moist towelette. Try using baby wipes with aloe vera, which clean and leave a fresh odor. Be sure to dry the area well.

some conjecture as to whether the d'Eresbys actually obtained two Pugs from a Russian tightrope walker, or whether they received a dog from a Hungarian countess who lived in Vienna. Nevertheless, the Willoughby Pugs, and indeed the Morrison Pugs, played a very important part in the breed's early development in Britain. It has been suggested that dogs of the Willoughby kennel came directly from the royal kennels of Queen Charlotte. In

time the two strains came together and so, to a certain extent, lost their individuality, though even today the distinctive bloodlines show through occasionally.

Although the story does not necessarily have foundation, well-known fawn-colored Pugs named Lamb and Moss featured prominently in the breed's history. Their parents allegedly were captured during the siege of the Summer Palace in China in 1860 and were brought to England by the Marquis of Wellesley, where they were given to Mrs. St. John. Some facts about this pair do not quite agree with history, but these two dogs were the parents of Click, one of the most important Pugs in the breed's history. Click was an invaluable stud, producing some very good females, and he also had a great bearing on the breed in the United States.

The little Pug awoke, his button ears twitching. Something wasn't right.

The Dutch camp was usually quiet in the dead of night, but in the distance he heard the faint sound of people entering the camp. They were strangers! He uttered a sharp bark, and his master rolled over. The sounds came closer. He barked again and again, pawing at the man's face.

Finally, William, Prince of Orange, sat up. Now he heard the sounds of fighting as his men encountered the Spanish soldiers infiltrating their camp at Hermigny. He swore. Grabbing the little Pug, named Pompey, he ran outside. A horse was always ready for him, in case of emergency, and he mounted quickly. Wrapping Pompey in his cloak, they rode into the darkness, evading capture.

Nevermore, William declared, would he sleep without one of these faithful dogs by his side. The breed became known as the official dog of the House of Orange, and a carving of Pompey on William's tomb in Delft Cathedral memorializes the Pug's bravery.

A little more than a century later, Pugs were still popular with the royal house of Holland. When William II of Holland and his wife the English princess Mary sailed from Holland to ascend the English throne in 1688 (after the death of Mary's brother, Charles II), they were accompanied by their Pugs.

Not surprisingly to those who know it, the Pug is still a popular companion today. The breed is loved not only for its loyalty but also for its unusual looks.

JOIN OUR ONLINE Pug Club

Just how quickly will your Pug puppy grow?
Go to Club Pug and download a growth chart. You also can see your pup's age in human years; the old standard of multiplying your dog's age by seven isn't quite accurate. Log onto **DogChannel.com/ Club-Pug** and click on "downloads."

BLACK PUGS

In 1877, black was considered a new color in the breed. Again, there has always been debate as to the actual origin of Lady Brassey's black Pugs, but she certainly exhibited some black dogs at Britain's Maidstone Show in 1886. One dog named Jack Spratt may have been acquired by Lady Brassey on her short trip to China.

Although black was claimed to be a new color, William Hogarth's paintings that blacks existed before then. Hogarth's *House of Cards*, painted in 1730, depicts a black Pug. A hundred years later, Queen Victoria owned a black Pug marked with white. The latter, though, may have been brought into England, perhaps as a gift to the queen from China.

It's believed that black Pugs were bred for many years earlier in England, but because they had been bred from fawn-colored Pugs, they were considered mutations and destroyed at birth. It is also possible that these blacks were not true black Pugs (ebonies), but were smuts (dark fawn Pugs), so they were not considered attractive.

In 1896 efforts were made to show the black Pug as an English-made variety, but despite considerable support this was not allowed. There was a very well-known black Pug who was known as the "singing Pug." Apparently, when given a chord on the piano, or by humming, he could pick up the note and sing. The black Pug certainly had his admirers, and in 1900, two were reported as having been sold to fanciers in New York for a sum totaling about $500, a lot of money at the time.

THE PUG IN ART

It is through art that we can best see the breed's place in the household and the evolution of the modern Pug. The earliest visual records of Pugs come courtesy of the French royal court. A fawn Pug, much like the ones we see today, appears in a family portrait of Louix XIV and his children, painted in 1713 or 1714. Louis XV commissioned a painting of a Pug in 1730. Many artists have incorporated the charming little Pug breed into their artworks, and from these paintings we have a good indication of the quality of dogs at the time. Franciso de Goya, a Spanish court painter, portrayed some lovely examples of the breed, and from these paintings, we can tell that the quality of the breed in Spain was high.

The most famous Pug painting is perhaps William Hogarth's 1745 self-portrait: *The Painter and His Pug* (which hangs in the Tate Gallery). Hogarth's dog, Trump, looks more like a white Bulldog than the Pug we know today. Forty years later, Goya immortalized the Marquesa de Pontejos and her Pug in an oil painting that can be found in Washington, D.C.'s National Gallery of Art. The Marquesa's dog, like that of Louis IV, also closely resembles the Pugs of today.

Renowned animal painter Philip Reinagle portrayed the charming Pug in his work, too. Many early dog books include engravings of this adorable breed, though not all of them have been well thought of by breed enthusiasts. Although there are many other portrayals of note, *Blonde and Brunette*, painted by Charles Burton Barber in 1879, is a favorite, and depicts a young lady engrossed in her book while her Pug rests comfortably in her arm.

In the mid- to late 19th century, paintings of Pugs more frequently begin to show a dog that resembles the modern breed. Still, there are differences. *Pug*, by B.A. Howe, circa 1850, shows a Pug with tightly cropped ears, a style that didn't go out of fashion until 1895, when it was outlawed in Britain as inhumane, thanks in part to Queen Victoria.

Art also shows us that problems with obesity aren't new to the Pug. John Emms' portrait of Punch, circa 1890, shows a slightly overweight Pug. Punch is also an example of the breed's evolution, having

Fawn-colored Pugs are favorites of owners and artists!

much shorter legs that had been developed by that time.

Most of the Pugs portrayed in artwork are fawn-colored, but there's one picture of a black Pug from Queen Victoria's kennel. The dog has a white blaze on his chest, which was common in black Pugs of the time (1895).

Meissen, or Dresden, porcelain is also famed for its portrayal of the Pug. Indeed, the Pug ranks among one of the most popular breeds of dog portrayed in porcelain and other collectable items. Most of those from the 18th century fetch very high prices, and even those from the 19th century are increasingly scarce. Sometimes such renderings are discovered of Pugs with cropped ears, and many have bells around their collars, making them even more charming.

NOTABLE & QUOTABLE *Pugs were bred to be companion dogs, and thus thrive on attention and affection from people.*

—*breeder J. Candy Schlieper of Tipp City, Ohio*

THE PUG COMES TO AMERICA

Although we lack documentation on the arrival of the first Pugs to the United States, we do know that some dogs were in the country shortly after the Civil War, which ended in 1865. The breed gained attention because of its uniqueness and, during the 1880s, many Pugs were shown in dog shows. The breed gained recognition from the American Kennel Club in 1885 and was classified in the Toy Group, as it is in other countries around the world.

The breed fell into relative obscurity at the turn of the 20th century as other breeds gained favor, many of which were "exotic imports" at the time. Breeders on the East Coast began stirring up interest in the Pug again, and by 1931, a club was formed. Twenty years later, the Pug Dog Club of America, the current parent club for the breed, was established as the Pug's principal promoter and protector in the United States.

Since those decades, the Pug has remained a popular breed, frequently seen in the show ring and counted among the top twenty breeds according the AKC's registration statistics. Although the Pug is not as flashy and intense as other top contenders in the Toy Group, including his Chinese relatives, the Pekingese and Shih Tzu, the breed does well in conformation shows and has racked up an impressive number of Best in Show awards over the years.

HOW THE PUG GOT HIS NAME

Throughout history, Pugs have been called by many names. In China, Pug-type dogs with short coats and wrinkled foreheads were known as *Lo-Sze*, and it was probably these dogs that gave rise to today's Pug.

Because of his body contour, wrinkled head and association with Holland, the early Pug in Europe was known as the Dutch mastiff, or sometimes the dwarf mastiff. In the early 18th century, the breed was sometimes called the Dutch Pug.

Popular pets of the 17th and 18th centuries included not only the little Asian dogs but also marmoset monkeys. The two animals bore a resemblance to each other, and the monkeys, which were known as Pugs, may have given their name to the dog breed. The word *pugg* or *pugge* was also used as a term of endearment during this time.

Dog authority Stonehenge suggested that the name came from the Latin word *pugnus*, meaning "fist," because the shadow of a fist was considered to resemble the dog's profile.

Over the years, the Pug has carried a number of nicknames. In Holland, it's often known as the *mopshond*, from the Dutch word meaning "to grumble," a reference to its frowny face. The Germans call it mops, as well. Because of their facial masks, French Pugs were called carlins, a reference perhaps to an 18th-century French actor known for his role of Harlequin. In this country, members of the breed are affectionately known as Puggies, Pugglies, and Puglets.

it's a Fact

In **1981**, the first Pug ever to win the famous **Westminster Kennel Club** dog show was named **Ch. Dhandys Favorite Woodchuck**, owned by Robert A. Hauslohner. To date, "Chucky," as his friends called him, is the only Pug to receive this great honor.

Several theories about the origin of the Pug's name exist; one includes a monkey look-alike!

Before looking for a Pug puppy, it is essential that you are fully committed to the decision that a Pug is the right breed for you and your family. The Pug is a small breed but is quite a tough little character in body *and* personality. The short coat should not present any problems, but if you have anyone in your family who is prone to allergies, be sure that he will not be affected by a Pug's coat before you make your purchase. Even dogs with short coats shed hair to a certain extent. Regular brushing will limit the amount of hair floating around your home or on your carpets and furniture.

POTENTIAL PUG PEOPLE

Smart owners should set out to purchase the best Pug that they can possibly afford. The safest method of finding your puppy is to seek out a reputable breeder. This is suggested even if you are not looking for a show specimen. The novice breeders and pet owners who advertise at attractive prices in

According to the breed standard, acceptable Pug coat colors are apricot-fawn or black. The apricot-fawn colors, which include silver, should be decided so as to make the contrast complete between the color and the trace (a black line extending from the back of the head along the top of the back to the twist of the tail) and the mask.

the local newspapers are probably kind enough toward their dogs, but perhaps they don't have the expertise or facilities required to successfully raise these dogs. These pups are frequently not weaned correctly and are left with their mothers too long without any supplemental feeding. This lack of proper feeding can cause indigestion, rickets, weak bones, poor teeth, and other problems. Vet bills may soon distort initial savings into financial or, worse, emotional loss.

You want to find an established breeder, someone who's been breeding Pugs for at least ten years and who belongs to his local and national breed clubs. Such a breeder has demonstrated outstanding dog ethics and a strong commitment to the Pug breed. An established breeder will be happy to answer your many questions and will make you comfortable with your choice of the Pug, even being able to explain the subtle differences in temperament and behavior between individual dogs in his home. A good breeder will sell you a puppy at a fair price if, and only if, he determines that you are a suitable, worthy owner of his dogs. The breeder can be relied upon for advice, no matter what time of day or night, and will accept a puppy back, without questions, should you decide that this is not the right dog for you.

When choosing a breeder, reputation and qualifications are much more important than where the breeder is

located. A three- or four-hour drive to pick up a new family member should not be that inconvenient.

Choosing a breeder is an important first step in dog ownership. Fortunately, most Pug breeders are devoted to the breed and its well-being, though be aware that there are backyard Pug "breeders" out there who take advantage of the breed's popularity and the ignorance of many new dog purchasers. With a little research and knowledge, potential owners should have little problem finding a reputable breeder who doesn't live too far away. Start with your local all-breed kennel club or Pug club. The American Kennel Club can direct you to the club or clubs nearest you; visit them online at www.akc.org. The Pug Dog Club of America maintains a breeder-referral service and also can put you in touch with your local club. The PDCA can be found online at www.pugs.org

Did You Know?

Signs of a Good Breeder
When you visit a breeder, be on the lookout for:
- a clean, well-maintained facility
- no overwhelming odors
- overall impression of cleanliness
- socialized dogs and puppies

Choosing the right breeder is a crucial first step to buying a Pug.

NOTABLE & QUOTABLE

I have no preference for males or females. I like both and have raised, trained, and shown both. Most Pug folks who know me know I do have a color preference. I adore my blacks. I tell folks the fawns are great, but there is nothing like a black!

—Christine Dresser, D.V.M., and Pug enthusiast

Referrals are an excellent way to find a pup. If you see a Pug you like, find out where he came from. Ask about health problems and temperament, and ask how the breeder was easy to work with. If that breeder doesn't have a puppy for you, he may be able to refer you to someone with similar lines.

Potential owners are encouraged to attend dog shows, obedience trails, or some other kind of performance event to see Pugs in action, to meet the owners and handlers firsthand, and to get an idea of what Pugs look like outside a photographer's lens. New owners may be surprised to see how large a standard Pug male is, or how small a female is. There's nothing like seeing Pugs live and up close. Provided you approach the handlers or owners at dog shows when they are not very busy, most are willing to answer questions, recommend breeders, and give advice. Pug people love to talk about their favorite topic: Pugs!

MEET AND GREET

Now it's time to meet one or two breeders and their dogs. If the breeder has young puppies, he may not allow you to visit for a few weeks to ensure the dog's safety. Whether he has pups when you visit or not, never go from one kennel to another with-

out going home, showering, and changing clothes, including your shoes (or clean them thoroughly, and spray the bottoms and sides with a ten-percent bleach solution). It is extremely easy to transmit deadly infectious diseases and parasites from one kennel to another, even if everything looks clean.

Look around. Does the environment look and smell reasonably clean? Do all the dogs appear to be healthy, with clear eyes, trimmed toenails, and well-groomed coats? Do they have fresh water to drink and room to move and play? Does the breeder know every dog by name and each puppy as an individual? If the answer to any of these questions is no, look elsewhere. If the answers are yes, though, and you feel comfortable with this breeder and like his dogs—and he feels comfortable with you—you may soon be owned by a Pug pup.

SELECTING A PUPPY

Once you have contacted and met a breeder or two and made your choice about which breeder is best suited to your needs, it's

Did You Know?

Healthy puppies have clear eyes, shiny coats, and are playful and friendly.

An important factor in a puppy's long-term health and good temperament is the age he goes to his permanent home, which should be between eight and twelve weeks. This gives the pups plenty of time to develop immunity and bond with their mom.

When it comes to selecting the right Pug for you, meet the parents!

Questions to Expect

Be prepared for the breeder to ask you some questions, too.

1. Have you previously owned a Pug?

The breeder is trying to gauge how familiar you are with the breed. If you have never owned one, illustrate your knowledge of Pugs by telling the breeder about your research.

2. Do you have children? What are their ages?

Some breeders are wary about selling a small dog to families with younger chil-dren. This isn't a steadfast rule, and some breeders only insist on meeting the chil-dren to see how they handle puppies. It all depends on the breeder.

3. How long have you wanted a Pug?

This helps a breeder know if this purchase is an impulse buy, or a carefully thought-out decision. Buying on impulse is one of the biggest mistakes owners can make. Be patient.

Join Club Pug to get a complete list of questions a breeder should ask you. Click on "downloads" at:
DogChannel.com/Club-Pug

Male and female Pugs are generally equal with only subtle personality and size differences.

time to visit the litter. Many top breeders have waiting lists, and sometimes new owners have to wait as long as two years for a puppy. If you are really committed to the breeder you've selected, then you will wait (and hope for an early arrival!). If not, you may have to resort to your second- or third-choice breeder. Don't be too anxious, however. If the breeder doesn't have anyone interested in his puppies, there is probably a good reason.

Because breeding a Pug is a delicate matter, and breeders must always test their breeding stock before producing a litter, most breeders do not expect a litter every season, or, for that matter, every year. Patience is a Pug virtue. The wait is worth it as you'll get a healthier and better socialized dog.

You are likely to be choosing a Pug as a pet, so select a puppy that is friendly and attractive. Pugs generally have small litters,

I have found the male dogs to be more people oriented, more underfoot, more clinging, and companionable. The females tend to be more alert and aloof; that doesn't mean they don't want attention. Females tend to be better at alerting when something is unusual within their home and boundaries.—Marcy Heathman, breeder from San Antonio, Texas

With the popularity of Pugs, shelters and rescue groups across the country are often inundated with sweet, loving examples of the breed—

from the tiniest puppies to senior dogs, petite females to blocky males. Often, to get the Pug of your dreams, it takes just a journey to the local shelter. Or perhaps you could find your ideal dog waiting patiently in the arms of a foster parent at a nearby rescue group. It just takes a bit of effort, patience, and a willingness to find the right dog for your family, not just the cutest dog on the block.

The perks of owning a Pug are plentiful: companionship, unconditional love, true loyalty, and laughter, just to name a few. So why choose the adoption option? You literally are saving a life!

Owners of adopted dogs swear they're more grateful and loving than any dog they've owned before. It's almost as if they knew what dire fate awaited them, and are so thankful to you. Pugs, known for their people-pleasing personalities, seem to embody this mentality whole-heartedly when they're rescued. And they want to give something back.

Another perk: Almost all adopted dogs come fully vetted, with proper medical treatment, vaccinations, medicine, as well as being spayed or neutered. Some are even licensed and microchipped.

Don't disregard older dogs, thinking the only good pair-up is you and a puppy. Adult Pugs are more established behaviorally and personality-wise, helping to better mesh their characteristics with yours in this game of matchmaker. Puppies are always high in demand, so if you open your options to include adult dogs, you'll have a better chance of adopting quickly. Plus, adult dogs are often house-trained, more calm, chew-proof, and don't need to be taken outside in the middle of the night. Five times. In the rain.

The Pug Dog Club of America offers rescue support information (www.pugs.org) or log onto Petfinder.com (www.petfinder.com). The site's searchable database enables you to find a Pug puppy in your area who needs a break in the form of a compassionate owner like you.

averaging three to five puppies (though larger litters are sometimes known), so selection may be limited once you have located a desirable litter. While the basic structure of the breed has little variation, the temperament may present trouble in certain strains. Beware of the shy or overly aggressive puppy; be especially conscious of the nervous Pug pup. Don't let sentiment or emotion trap you into buying the runt of the litter.

The gender of your puppy is largely a matter of personal taste. Male Pugs show great kindness toward female Pugs, and both sexes are extremely placid and laid-back. The difference in size is noticeable but slight. Coloration is not the most important consideration when selecting a Pug, either. Remember that it will be more difficult to find a good silver pup, as the apricot-fawns are most numerous. The black Pugs, unique in their own right, possess single coats, which may be preferable for the allergic owner.

Breeders commonly allow visitors to see the litter by around the fifth or sixth week,

and Pug puppies leave for their new homes around the tenth week. Breeders who permit their puppies to leave early are more interested in your money than their puppies' well-being. Puppies need to learn the rules of the pack from their mothers, and most dams continue teaching the pups manners and dos and don'ts until around the eighth week. Breeders spend significant amounts of time with the Pug toddlers so that they are able to interact with the "other species," i.e., humans. Given the long history that dogs and humans have, bonding between the two species is natural but must be nurtured. A well-bred Pug pup wants nothing more than to be near you and please you.

ESSENTIAL PAPERWORK

Make sure the breeder has proper papers to go with the puppy of your choice.

Contract: You should receive a copy of the purchase contract you signed when you bought your puppy. The contract should specify the purchase price, health guarantee, spay/neuter requirements by a certain age,

Breeder Q&A

Here are some questions you should ask a breeder and the preferred answers you want.

Q. How often do you have litters available?

A. The answer you want to hear is "once or twice a year" or "occasionally" because a breeder who doesn't have litters all that often is probably more concerned with the quality of his puppies, rather than with producing a lot of puppies to make money.

Q. What kinds of health problems have you had with your Pugs?

A. Beware of a breeder who says, "none." Every breed has health issues. For Pugs, some health problems include Pug Dog Encephalitis, eye diseases, patellar luxation, and ideopathic epilepsy.

Get a complete list of questions to ask a Pug breeder—and the correct answers—on Club Pug. Log onto **DogChannel.com/Club-Pug** and click on "downloads."

Always opt for the friendly and healthy Pug pup, to avoid problems in the future.

it's a Fact

Food intolerance is the inability of the dog to completely digest certain foods. Puppies that may have done very well on their mother's milk may not do well on cow's milk. The result of this food intolerance may be loose bowels, passing gas, and stomach pains. These are the only obvious symptoms of food intolerance, and that makes diagnosis difficult.

and conditions to return the pup if you find you can't keep her for any reason.

Registration Papers: If the breeder said that the puppy's parents were registered with the American Kennel Club or United Kennel Club, you should receive an application form to register your puppy—or at the very least, a signed bill of sale that you can use to register your puppy. The bill of sale should include the puppy's breed, date of birth, sex, registered names of the parents, litter number, the breeder's name, date of sale, and the seller's signature. Registration allows your Pug puppy to compete in ken-

Get your Pug used to new people as soon as you bring him home.

Ask for a copy of your Pug's pedigree from the breeder; the apple doesn't fall far from the tree!

nel club-sanctioned events such as agility, obedience, and rally trials. Registration fees support research and other activities sponsored by the organization. If your intention is to show your Pug, be sure not to purchase a puppy that the breeder promises is "AKC registration eligible" because it's unlikely he will be; only fully registered dogs can participate in AKC conformation shows.

Pedigree: The breeder should include a copy of your puppy's family tree, listing your puppy's parents, grandparents, and beyond, depending on how many genera-

Did You Know?

Properly bred puppies come from parents that were selected based upon their genetic disease profile. Their mothers should have been vaccinated, free of all internal and external parasites, and properly nourished. For these reasons, a visit to the veterinarian who cared for the dam is recommended. The mother can pass on disease resistance to her puppies, which can last for eight to ten weeks.

tions the pedigree includes. It also lists any degrees or titles that those relatives have earned. Look for indications that the dog's ancestors were active and successful in dog sports. The information that a pedigree provides can help you understand more about the physical conformation and/or behavioral accomplishments of your puppy's family. Usually the quality of the pedigree dictates the price of the puppy, so expect to pay a higher price for a higher quality puppy. However, chances are that you will be rewarded by the quality of life that you and your pedigreed puppy will enjoy!

Health Records: You should receive from the breeder a copy of your puppy's health records, including his date of birth, visits to the vet and immunizations. Bring the health records to your vet when you take your puppy in for his first checkup, which should take place within a few days of his arrival in your household. The records will become part of your puppy's permanent health file.

Care Instructions: Finally, the Pug breeder should provide you with written instructions on basic puppy care.

BUYER BEWARE

As with any breed of dog, a litter occasionally will have puppies that are below or above the breed's desired size range. Overly big Pugs can make great pets; however, their size is a serious fault in the show ring. Extremely tiny Pugs generally aren't shown because quality breeders feel the more miniscule the Pug, the higher the risk of health problems that can be passed along in their breeding programs.

Any deviation from the breed standard actually makes the Pug less valuable, but don't despair—this dog can be a great pet-quality pup (one that has minor cosmetic flaws that prevent him from competing in conformation). And, often extremely unusual coloring can indicate that the puppy is actually a mix of breeds rather than a true purebred Pug.

Signs of a Healthy Puppy

Here are a few things you should look for when selecting a puppy from a litter.

1. **NOSE:** It should be slightly moist to the touch, but there shouldn't be excessive discharge. The puppy should not be sneezing or sniffling persistently.

2. **SKIN AND COAT:** Your Pug puppy's coat should be soft and shiny, without flakes or excessive shedding. Watch out for patches of missing hair, redness, bumps or sores. The pup should have a pleasant smell. Check for parasites, such as fleas or ticks.

3. **BEHAVIOR:** A healthy Pug puppy may be sleepy, but he should not be lethargic. A healthy pup will be playful at times, not isolated in a corner. You should see occasional bursts of energy and interaction with littermates. When it's mealtime, a healthy pup will take an interest in his food.

There are more signs to look for when picking out the perfect Pug puppy for you. Download the list at **DogChannel.com/Club-Pug**

Keep a close eye on your puppy's behavior —a healthy puppy will be energetic and playful, not lethargic.

CHAPTER 4

HOME

ESSENTIALS

Pug puppies are tiny, fragile, and vulnerable, but this doesn't make them any less interested in living the puppy life. Is it possible to let your Pug enjoy being a dog without risking life and limb? Their natural curiosity can border on recklessness, which means puppy-proofing your humble abode from the ground up.

How you prepare your home will depend on how much freedom your dog will be allowed. A smart owner will designate a couple of rooms (without stairs) for his new Pug puppy.

In order for a puppy to grow into a stable, well-adjusted dog, he has to feel comfortable in his surroundings. Remember, he is leaving the warmth and security of his mother and littermates, as well as the familiarity of the only place he has ever known, so it is important to make his transition to your home—his new home—as easy as possible.

PUPPY-PROOFING

Aside from making sure that your Pug will be comfortable in your home, you also have to ensure that your home is safe, which means taking the proper precautions to keep

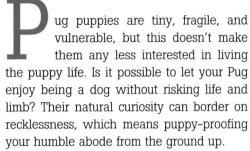

it's a Fact

Dangers lurk indoors and out. Keep your curious Pug from investigating your shed and garage. Antifreeze and fertilizers, such as those you would use for roses, will kill a Pug. Keep these items on high shelves that are out of reach for your small dog.

A well-stocked toy box should contain three main categories of toys.

1. **action** (anything that you can throw or roll and get things moving)
2. **distraction** (durable toys that make dogs work for a treat)
3. **comfort** (soft, stuffed little "security blankets"

your pup away from things that are dangerous for him.

Puppy-proof your home inside and out before brining your Pug home for the first time. Place breakables out of reach. If he is limited to certain places within the house, keep potentially dangerous items in off-limit areas. If your Pug is going to spend time in a crate, make sure that there is nothing near it that he can reach if he sticks his curious little nose or paws through the openings.

The outside of your home must also be safe. Your pup will want to run and explore the yard, and he should be granted that freedom—as long as you are there to supervise him. Do not let a fence give you a false sense of security; you would be surprised how crafty (and persistent) a dog can be in figuring out how to dig under a fence or squeeze his way through small holes. And because of his small size, your Pug can slip through the tiniest of holes. The remedy is to make the fence well embedded into the ground. Be sure to repair or secure any gaps in the fence. Check the fence periodically to ensure that it is in good shape and make repairs as needed; a very determined pup may work on the same spot until he is able to get through.

The following are a few common problem areas to watch out for in the home.

Comfort is key in making your new Pug pup feel right at home.

Pug pups are *very* curious, so be sure to keep unsafe objects out of paw's reach.

■ **Electrical cords and wiring:** No electrical cord or wiring is safe. Many office-supply stores sell products to keep wires gathered under computer desks, as well as products that prevent office chair wheels (and puppy teeth) from damaging electrical cords. If you have exposed cords and wires, these products aren't very expensive and can be used to keep a pup out of trouble.

■ **Trash cans:** Don't waste your time trying to train your Pug not to get into the trash. Simply put the garbage behind a cabinet door and use a child-safe lock if necessary. Dogs love bathroom trash (i.e., cotton balls, cotton swabs, used razors, dental floss, etc.), which consists of items that are all extremely dangerous! Put this trash can in a cabinet under the sink and make sure you always shut the door to the bathroom.

■ **Household cleaners:** Make sure your Pug puppy doesn't have access to any of these deadly chemicals. Keep them behind closed cabinet doors, using child-safe locks if necessary.

■ **Pest control sprays and poisons:** Chemicals to control ants or other pests

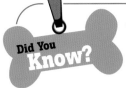

Did You Know?

Carrying a dog too much can make him fearful toward people or overly possessive of his owner, prompting a threatening demeanor. Laughing at, praising, or otherwise encouraging this poor behavior because it's "cute," ensures it continues. Insist your Pug exhibit the same manners expected in a large dog.

should never be used in the house, if possible. Your pup doesn't have to directly ingest these poisons to become ill; if the Pug steps in the poison, he can experience toxic effects by licking his paws. Roach motels and other poisonous pest traps are also evidently yummy to dogs, so don't drop these behind couches or cabinets; if there's room for a roach motel, there's room for a determined Pug.

■ **Fabric:** Here's one you might not think about: Some puppies have a habit of licking blankets, upholstery, rugs, or carpets. Though this habit seems fairly innocuous, over time the fibers from the upholstery or carpet can accumulate in the dog's stomach and cause a blockage. If you see your dog licking these items, remove the item or prevent him from having contact with it.

■ **Prescriptions, painkillers, supplements, and vitamins:** Keep all medications in a cabinet. Also, be very careful when taking your prescription medications, supplements, or vitamins: How often have you dropped a pill? With a Pug, you can be assured that your puppy will be in between your legs and will snarf up the pill before you can even start to say "No!" Dispense your own pills carefully and without your Pug present.

■ **Miscellaneous loose items:** If it's not bolted to the floor, your puppy is likely to give the item a taste test. Socks, coins, children's toys, game pieces, cat bell balls—you name it; if it's on the floor, it's worth a try. Make sure the floors in your home are picked up and free of clutter.

FAMILY INTRODUCTIONS

Everyone in the house will be excited about the puppy's homecoming and will want to pet and play with him, but it is best to make the introduction low-key so as not to overwhelm the puppy. He already will be apprehensive. It is the first time he has been separated from his mother, littermates, and the breeder, and the ride to your home is likely to be the first time he has been in a car. The last thing you want to do is smother your Pug, as this will only frighten him further. This is not to say that human contact is not extremely necessary at this stage because this is the time when a connection between the pup and his human family is formed. Gentle petting and soothing words should help console your Pug, as well as just putting him down and letting him explore on his own (under your watchful eye, of course).

Welcome your Pug in a calm, soothing, low-key manner to put him at ease.

The first thing you should always do before your puppy comes home is to lie on the ground and look around. You want to be able to see everything your puppy is going to see. For the puppy, the world is a big chew toy.

—Cathleen Stamm, rescue volunteer in San Diego, Calif.

Your pup may approach the family members or may busy himself with exploring for a while. Gradually, each person should spend some time with the pup, one at a time, crouching down to get as close to the Pug's level as possible and letting him sniff their hands before petting him gently. He definitely needs human attention, and he needs to be touched; this is how to form an immediate bond. Just remember that the pup is experiencing a lot of things for the first time, at the same time. There are new people, new noises, new smells, and new things to investigate, so be gentle, be affectionate, and be as comforting as you can be.

PUP'S FIRST NIGHT HOME

You have traveled home with your new charge safely in his crate. He may have already been to the vet for a thorough check-

Did You Know?

Everyone who rides in your car has to buckle up—even your little Pug! Your dog can travel in the car inside his crate, or you can use a doggie seat belt. These look like harnesses that attach to your car's seat-belt system.

up—he's been weighed, his papers examined, perhaps he's even been vaccinated and wormed as well. Your Pug has met and licked the whole family, including the excited children and the less-than-happy cat. He's explored his area, his new bed, the yard, and anywhere else he's permitted. He's eaten his first meal at home and relieved himself in the proper place. Your Pug has heard lots of new sounds, smelled new

friends, and seen more of the outside world than ever before.

This was just the first day! He's worn out and is ready for bed—or so you think! Remember, this is your puppy's first night to sleep alone. His mother and littermates are no longer at paw's length, and he's scared, cold, and lonely. Be reassuring to your new family member. This is not the time to spoil your Pug and give in to his inevitable whining.

Puppies whine. They whine to let others know where they are and hopefully to get company out of it. Place your Pug puppy in his new bed or crate in his room and close the door. Mercifully, he may fall asleep without a peep. If the inevitable occurs, ignore the whining; he is fine. Do not give in and visit your Pug puppy. He will fall asleep eventually.

Many breeders recommend placing a piece of bedding from his former home in his new bed so that he recognizes the scent of his littermates. Others still advise placing a hot water bottle in his bed for warmth. The latter may be a good idea provided the pup doesn't attempt to suckle; he'll get good and wet and may not fall asleep so fast.

Your Pug's first night can be somewhat terrifying for him *and* his new family. Remember that you set the tone of nighttime at your house. Unless you want to play with your pup every night at 10 p.m., midnight, and 2 a.m., don't initiate the habit. Your family will thank you, and so will your pup!

SMART TIP!

9-1-1! If you don't know whether the plant or food or "stuff" your Pug just ate is toxic to dogs, you can call the ASPCA's Animal Poison Control Center (888-426-4435). Be prepared to provide your puppy's age and weight, his symptoms—if any—and how much of the plant, chemical, or substance he ingested, as well as how long ago you think he came into contact with the substance. The ASPCA charges a consultation fee for this service.

Don't give into a Pug's whining —it will trigger a bad habit.

A Pug might soon become your favorite shopping partner.

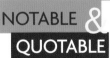

NOTABLE & QUOTABLE

Playing with toys from puppyhood encourages good behavior and social skills throughout the dog's life. A happy, playful dog is a content and well-adjusted one. Also, because all puppies chew to soothe their gums and help loosen puppy teeth, dogs should always have easy access to several different toys.—dog trainer and author Harrison Forbes of Savannah, Tenn.

Keep a crate in your vehicle and take your Pug along when you visit the drive-through at the bank or your favorite fast-food restaurant. He can watch interactions, hear interesting sounds, and maybe garner a dog treat.

SHOPPING FOR A PUG

It's fun shopping for a new puppy. From training to feeding and sleeping to playing, your new Pug will need a few items to make life comfy, easy, and fun. Be prepared and visit your local pet-supply store before you bring home your new family member.

◆ **Collar and ID tag:** Accustom your dog to wearing a collar the first day you bring him home. Not only will a collar and ID tag help your pup in the event that he becomes lost, but collars are also an important training tool. If your Pug gets into trouble, the collar will act as a handle, helping you divert him to a more appropriate behavior. Make sure the collar fits snugly enough so that your Pug cannot wriggle out of it, but is loose enough so that it will not be uncomfortably tight around his neck. You should be able to fit a finger between the pup and the collar. Collars come in many styles, but for starting out, a simple buckle collar with an easy-release snap works great.

◆ **Leash:** For training or just for taking a stroll down the street, a leash is your Pug's vehicle to explore the outside world. Like collars, leashes come in a variety of styles and materials. A six-foot nylon leash is a popular choice because it is lightweight and durable. As your pup grows and gets used to walking on the leash, you may want to purchase a flexible leash. These leads allow you to extend the length to give the dog a broader area to explore or to shorten the length to keep the dog closer to you.

◆ **Bowls:** Your Pug will need two bowls: one for water and one for food. You may

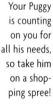

Your Puggy is counting on you for all his needs, so take him on a shopping spree!

A well-fitting collar and ID tag are must-have items for your puppy. Make sure you purchase ones that are appropriately sized.

want two sets of bowls, one for inside and one for outside, depending on where the dog will be fed and where he will be spending time. Bowls should be sturdy enough so that they don't tip over easily. (Most have reinforced bottoms that prevent tipping.) Bowls usually are made of metal, ceramic, or plastic, and should be easy to clean.

◆ **Crate:** A multipurpose crate serves as a bed, house-training tool, and travel carrier. It also is the ideal doggie den—a bedroom of sorts—that your Pug can retire to when he wants to rest or just needs a break. The crate should be large enough for your Pug to stand in, turn around, and lie down. You don't want any more room than this—especially if you're planning on using the crate to house-train your dog—because he will eliminate in one corner and lie down in another. Get a crate that is big enough for your dog when he is an adult. Then use dividers to limit the space when he's a puppy.

◆ **Bed:** A plush doggie bed will make sleeping and resting more comfortable for your Pug. Dog beds come in all

shapes, sizes, and colors, but your dog just needs one that is soft and large enough for him to stretch out on. Because puppies and rescue dogs often don't come house-trained, it's helpful to buy a bed that can be washed easily. If your Pug will be sleeping in a crate, a nice crate pad and a small blanket that he can "burrow" in will help him feel more at home. Replace the blanket if it becomes ragged and starts to fall apart because your Pug's nails could get caught in it.

◆ **Gate:** Similar to those used for toddlers, gates help keep your Pug confined to one room or area when you can't supervise him. Gates also work to keep your dog out of areas you don't want him in. Gates are available in many styles. For Pugs, make sure the one you choose has openings small enough so your tiny puppy can't squeeze through the bars or any openings.

◆ **Toys:** Keep your dog occupied and entertained by providing him with an array of fun toys. Teething puppies like to chew—in fact, chewing is a physical need for pups as they are teething—and everything from your shoes to the leather couch to the Oriental rug are fair game. Divert your Pug's chewing instincts with durable toys like bones made of nylon or hard rubber.

Toys are just as fun as treats—when your Pug behaves reward him with a squeak toy.

SMART TIP!

When you are unable to watch your Pug puppy, put him in a crate or an exercise pen on an easily cleanable floor. If he does have an accident on carpeting, clean it completely and meticulously, so thatit doesn't forever smell like his potty accident.

Other fun toys include rope toys, treat-dispensing toys, and balls. Make sure the toys and bones don't have small parts that could break off and be swallowed, causing your dog to choke. Stuffed toys can become destuffed, and an overly excited puppy may ingest the stuffing or the squeaker. Check your Pug's toys regularly and replace them if they become frayed or show signs of wear.

◆ **Cleaning supplies:** Until your Pug pup is house-trained, you will be doing a lot of cleaning. Accidents will occur, which is acceptable in the beginning because the puppy doesn't know any better. All you can do is be prepared to clean up any accidents. Old rags, towels, newspapers, and a stain-and-odor remover are good to have on hand.

BEYOND THE BASICS

The items previously discussed are the bare necessities. You will find out what else you need as you go along—grooming supplies, flea/tick protection, etc. These things will vary depending on your situation, but it is important that you have everything you need to make your Pug comfortable in his new home.

Soon enough, your new Pug will be just another member of the family!

Some ordinary household items make great toys for your Pug—as long you make sure they are safe. You will find a list of homemade toys at **DogChannel.com/Club-Pug**

SUCCESSFUL

HOUSE-TRAINING

Small dogs seem to offer a challenge when it comes to house-training. There are several reasons for this: It's easier to miss a small dog's "I gotta go" signals; smaller dog, smaller mess; messes are easier to miss; etc. It may also be true that because a small dog's organs are smaller, they don't have the capacity to hold it for as long as a big dog.

Smart owners know that successful house-training means total supervision and management—crates, tethers, exercise pens, and leashes—until the dog has developed substrate preferences for outside surfaces (grass, gravel, concrete) instead of carpet, tile, or hardwood, and knows that potty happens outside.

IN THE BEGINNING

For the first two to three weeks of a puppy's life, his mother helps the pup to eliminate. She keeps the whelping box or "nest area" clean. When pups begin to walk around and eat on their own, they choose where they eliminate. You can train your puppy to relieve himself wherever you choose, but this must be somewhere suitable.

it's a Fact Ongoing house-training difficulties may indicate your puppy has a health problem, warranting a veterinary checkup. A urinary infection, parasites, a virus, and other nasty issues greatly affect your puppy's ability to hold pee or poop.

Bear in mind from the outset that when your puppy is old enough to go out in public places, any canine deposits must be removed at once. You will always have to carry a small plastic bag or "poop-scoop."

Outdoor training includes such surfaces as grass, soil, and concrete. Indoor training usually means training your dog on newspaper. When deciding on the surface and location,

be sure it is going to be permanent. Training your dog to grass and then changing your mind two months later is extremely difficult for dog and owner.

Next, choose the cue you will use each and every time you want your puppy to void. "Let's go," "hurry up," and "potty" are examples of cues commonly used by dog owners.

Get in the habit of giving the puppy your chosen relief command before you take him out. That way, when he becomes an adult, you will be able to determine if he wants to go out when you ask him. A confirmation will be signs of interest, such as wagging his tail, watching you intently, going to the door, etc.

LET'S START WITH THE CRATE

Clean animals by nature, dogs keenly dislike soiling where they sleep and eat. This

Did You Know?

Cleaning accidents properly with an enzyme solution will dramatically reduce the time it takes to house-train your dog because he won't be drawn back to the same areas.

fact makes a crate a useful tool for house-training. When purchasing a new crate, consider that one correctly sized will allow adequate room for an adult dog to stand full-height, lie on his side without scrunching, and turn around easily. If debating plastic versus wire crates, short-haired breeds sometimes prefer the warmer, draft-blocking quality of plastic, while furry dogs often like the cooling airflow of a wire crate.

Some crates come equipped with a movable wall that reduces the interior size to provide enough space for your puppy to stand, turn, and lie down, while not allowing room to soil one end and sleep in the other. The problem is that if your puppy goes potty in the crate anyway, the divider forces him to lie in his own excrement.

This can work against you by desensitizing your puppy against his normal, instinctive revulsion to resting where he's eliminated. If scheduling permits you or a responsible family member to clean the crate soon after it's soiled, feel free to use this aid, as limiting crate size does encourage your puppy to hold it. Otherwise, give him enough room to move away from an unclean area until he's better able to control his elimination.

Needless to say, not every puppy adheres to this guideline. If your puppy moves along at a faster pace, thank your lucky stars. Should he progress slower, accept it and remind yourself that he'll improve. Be aware that pups frequently hold it longer at night than during the day. Just because your puppy sleeps for six or more hours through the night, does not mean he can hold it that long during the more active daytime hours.

One last bit of advice on the crate: Place it in the corner of a normally trafficked room, such as the family room or kitchen. Social and curious by nature, dogs like to feel

Pay close attention to your Pug's "I-gotta-go" signals.

included in family happenings. Creating a quiet retreat by putting the crate in an unused area may seem like a good idea, but results in your puppy feeling insecure and isolated. Watching his people pop in and out of the crate room reassures your puppy that he's not forgotten.

A PUPPY'S NEEDS

Your Pug pup needs to relieve himself after play periods, after each meal, after he has been sleeping, and any time he indicates that he's looking for a place to pee or poop.

The urinary and intestinal tract muscles of very young puppies are not fully developed. Therefore, like human babies, pups need to relieve themselves often. Take your pup out every hour for an eight-week-old, for example, and always immediately after sleeping and eating. The older the puppy, the less often he will need to relieve himself. Finally, as a mature healthy adult, he will require only three to five relief trips per day.

HOUSING HELPS

Because the types of housing and control you provide for your puppy have a direct relationship on the success of house-training, consider the various aspects of both before beginning training.

Bringing a new puppy home and turning him loose in your house can be compared to turning a child loose in a sports arena and telling the child that the place is all his! The sheer enormity of the place would be too much for him to handle.

Instead, offer your puppy clearly defined areas where he can play, sleep, eat, and live. A room of the house where the family gathers is the most obvious choice. Puppies are social animals and need to feel a part of the pack right from the start. Hearing your voice, watching you while you are doing things, and smelling you nearby are all positive reinforcers that he is a member of your pack. Usually a family room, the kitchen, or a nearby adjoining breakfast area is ideal for providing safety and security for both puppy and owner.

Within that room, there should be a smaller area that the puppy can call his own. An alcove, a wire or fiberglass dog crate, or

Reward your pup with a high-value treat immediately after he potties to reinforce going in the proper location, then play for a short time afterward. This teaches that good things happen after pottying outside!—Victoria Schade, certified pet dog trainer, from Annandale, Va.

SMART TIP!

Toy dogs are notorious for being difficult to house-train. Some of the reasons stem from their early experiences. Dogs who are raised in pens where they're forced to potty inside tend to be indiscriminate about where they go later in life. In fact, as adults, dogs tend to prefer using the same type of surface they pottied on as puppies.

a fenced (not boarded!) corner from which he can view the activities of his new family will be fine. The size of the area or crate is the key factor here. The area must be large enough for the puppy to lie down and stretch out, but small enough so that he cannot relieve himself at one end and sleep at the other without coming into contact with his droppings before he is fully trained to relieve himself outside.

Dogs are, by nature, clean animals and will not remain close to their relief areas unless forced to do so. In those cases, they then become dirty dogs and usually remain that way for life.

The designated area should be lined with clean bedding and a toy. Water must always be available, in a nonspill container, once the dog is house-trained reliably.

IN CONTROL

By control, we mean helping your puppy to create a pattern that will be compatible to that of his human pack (you!). Just as we guide little children to learn our way of life, we must show the puppy when it is time to play, eat, sleep, exercise, and even entertain himself.

Your puppy should always sleep in his crate. He should also learn that, during times of household confusion and excessive human activity, such as at breakfast when family members are preparing for the day, he can play by himself in relative safety and comfort in his designated area. Each time you leave the puppy alone, he should understand exactly where he is to stay. Puppies are chewers. They cannot tell the difference between lamp cords, television wires, shoes,

or table legs. Chewing into a television wire, for example, can be fatal to the puppy, while a shorted wire can start a fire in the house.

If the puppy chews on the arm of the chair when he is alone, you will probably discipline him angrily when you get home.

Did You Know?

White vinegar is a good odor remover if you don't have any professional cleaners on hand; use one-quarter cup to one quart of water.

SMART TIP!

When proximity prevents you from going home at lunch or during periods when overtime crops up, make alternative arrangements for getting your puppy out. Hire a pet-sitting or walking service, or enlist the aid of an obliging neighbor willing to help.

He then makes the association that your coming home means that he is going to be punished. (He will not remember chewing the chair and is incapable of making the association of the discipline with his naughty deed.)

Other times of excitement, such as family parties, can be fun for the puppy, providing that he can view the activities from the security of his designated area. He is not underfoot and he is not being fed all sorts of tidbits that will probably cause him stomach distress, yet he still feels a part of the fun.

SCHEDULE A SOLUTION

A puppy should be taken to his relief area each time he is released from his designated area, after meals, after play sessions, and when he first awakens in the morning (at age eight weeks, this can mean at 5 a.m.!). The puppy will indicate that he's ready "to go" by circling or sniffing busily—do not misinterpret these signs. For a puppy less than ten weeks of age, a routine of taking him out every hour is necessary. As the puppy grows, he will be able to wait for longer periods of time.

Keep trips to his relief area short. Stay no more than five or six minutes and then return to the house. If he goes during that time, praise him lavishly, and

take him indoors immediately. If he does not, but he has an accident when you go back indoors, pick him up immediately, say "No! No!" and return to his relief area. Wait a few minutes, then return to the house again. Never hit a puppy or rub his face in urine or excrement when he has had an accident.

Once indoors, put the puppy in his crate until you have had time to clean up his accident. Then release him to the family area and watch him more closely than before. Chances are, his accident was a result of your not picking up his signal or waiting too long before offering him the opportunity to relieve himself. Never hold a grudge against the puppy for accidents.

Let the puppy learn that going outdoors means it is time to relieve himself, not to

10 House-training How-Tos

1. Decide where you want your Pug to eliminate. Take him there every time until he gets the idea. Pick a spot that's easy to access. Remember, puppies have very little time between "gotta go" and "oops."

2. Teach an elimination cue, such as "go potty" or "get busy." Say this every time you take your Pug to eliminate. Don't keep chanting the cue, just say it once or twice then keep quiet so you won't distract your dog.

3. Praise calmly when your dog eliminates, but stand there a little longer in case there's more.

4. Keep potty outings for potty only. Take the dog to the designated spot, tell him "go potty" and just stand there. If he needs to eliminate, he will do so within five minutes.

5. Don't punish for potty accidents—punishment can hinder progress. If you catch your Pug in the act indoors, verbally interrupt but don't scold. Gently carry or lead your pup to the approved spot, let him finish, then praise.

6. If it's too late to interrupt an accident, scoop the poop or blot up the urine afterward with a paper towel. Immediately take your Pug and his deposit (gently!) to the potty area.

Place the poop or trace of urine on the ground and praise the pup. If he sniffs at its waste, praise more. Let your Pug know you're pleased when his waste is in the proper area.

7. Keep track of when and where your Pug eliminates—that will help you anticipate potty times. Regular meals mean regular elimination, so feed your Pug scheduled, measured meals instead of free-feeding (leaving food available at all times).

8. Hang a bell on a sturdy cord from the doorknob. Before you open the door to take your Pug out for potty, shake the string and ring the bell. Most dogs soon realize the connection between the bell ringing and the door opening, then they'll try it out for themselves. Listen for that bell!

9. Dogs naturally return to re-soil where they've previously eliminated, so thoroughly clean up all accidents. Household cleaners usually will do the job, but special enzyme solutions may work better.

10. If the ground is littered with too much waste, your Pug may seek a cleaner place to eliminate. Scoop the potty area daily, leaving just one "reminder."

If your Pug makes a mistake, don't scold him; simply clean it up and try again. Patience is a virtue!

play. Once trained, he will be able to play indoors and out and still differentiate between the times for play versus the times for relief.

Help him develop regular hours for naps, being alone, playing by himself and just resting, all in his crate. Encourage him to entertain himself while you are busy with your activities. Let him learn that having you nearby is comforting, but it is not your main purpose in life to provide him with undivided attention.

Each time you put a pup in his own area, use the same command, whatever suits you best. Soon he will run to his crate or special area when he hears you say those words.

Crate-training provides safety for you, your puppy, and your home. It also provides the puppy with a feeling of security, and that helps the puppy achieve self-confidence and clean habits.

Remember that one of the primary ingredients in house-training your puppy is control. Regardless of your lifestyle, there will always be occasions when you will need to have a place where your dog can stay and be happy and safe. Crate-training is the answer for now and in the future.

A few key elements are really all you and your Pug need for a successful house-training method: consistency, frequency, praise, control, and supervision. By following these procedures with a normal, healthy puppy, you and your Pug will soon be past the stage of accidents and ready to move on to a full and rewarding life together.

Having house-training problems with your Pug? Ask other Pug owners for advice and tips. Log onto **DogChannel.com/Club-Pug** and click on "community."

EVERYDAY CARE

Your selection of a veterinarian should be based on personal recommendation for the doctor's skills with dogs, and, if possible, especially Pugs. If the vet is based nearby, it will be helpful because you might have an emergency or need to make multiple visits for treatments.

FIRST STEP: SELECT THE RIGHT VET

All licensed veterinarians are capable of dealing with routine medical issues such as infections and injuries, as well as the promotion of health (for example, by vaccinations). If the problem affecting your Pug is more complex, your vet will refer you to someone with more detailed knowledge of what is wrong. This usually will be a specialist who is a veterinary dermatologist, veterinary ophthalmologist, etc., whatever field you require.

Veterinary procedures are very costly and, as the treatments available improve, they are going to become more expensive. It is quite acceptable to discuss matters of cost with your vet; if there is more than one treatment option, cost may be a factor in deciding which route to take.

Smart owners will look for a veterinarian before they actually need one. For newbie pet owners, ideally start looking for a veterinarian a month or two before you bring home your new Pug puppy. That will give you time to meet candidate veterinarians, check out the condition of the clinic, meet the staff, and see who you feel most comfortable with. If you already have a Pug puppy, look sooner rather than later, preferably not in the midst of a veterinary health crisis.

Second, define the criteria that are important to you. Points to consider or investigate:

Convenience: Proximity to your home, extended hours, or drop-off services are helpful for people who work regular business hours, have a busy schedule, or don't want to drive far. If you have mobility issues, finding a vet who makes house calls or a service that provides pet transport might be particularly important.

Size: A one-person practice ensures that you will always be dealing with the same vet during each and every visit. "That person can really get to know you and your dog," says Bernadine Cruz, D.V.M., of Laguna Hills Animal Hospital in Laguna Hills, Calif. The downside, though, is that the sole practitioner does not have the immediate input of another vet, and if your vet becomes ill or takes time off, you are out of luck.

The multiple-doctor practice offers consistency if your Pug needs to come in unexpectedly on a day when your veterinarian isn't there. Additionally, your vet can quickly consult with his colleagues within the clinic if he's unsure about a diagnosis or a treatment.

If you find a veterinarian within that practice who you really like, you can make your appointments with that individual, establishing the same kind of bond that you would with the solo practitioner.

Appointment Policies: Some practices are strictly by-appointment only, which could minimize your wait time. However, if a sudden problem arises with your Pug and the veterinarians are booked up, they might not be able to squeeze your pet in that day. Some clinics are drop-in only—great for impromptu or crisis visits, but without scheduling may involve longer waits to see the next available veterinarian—whoever is open, not someone in particular. Some practices maintain an appointment schedule but also keep slots open throughout the day for walk-ins, offering the best of both worlds.

Basic vs. State-of-the-Art vs. Full Service: A practice with high-tech equipment offers greater diagnostic capabilities and treatment options, important for tricky or difficult cases. However, the cost of pricey equipment is passed along to the client, so you could pay more for routine procedures—the bulk of most pets' appointments. Some

Picking the right vet is one of the most important decisions you'll make for the lifelong health of your new family member. Make sure you ask the right questions to ensure that your vet is knowledgeable not only about dogs, but Pugs in particular. Download a list of questions to ask potential vets by logging on to **DogChannel.com/Club-Pug**—just click on "downloads."

practices offer boarding, grooming, training classes, and other services on the premises—conveniences some pet owners appreciate.

Fees and Payment Polices: How much is a routine office call? If there is a significant price difference, ask why. If you intend to carry health insurance on your Pug or want to pay by credit card, make sure the candidate clinic accepts those payment options.

FIRST VET VISIT

It is much easier, less costly, and more effective to practice preventive medicine than to fight bouts of illness and disease. Properly bred puppies of all breeds come from parents who were selected based upon their genetic disease profile. The puppies' mother should have been vaccinated, free of all internal and external par-

Overall, Pugs are a healthy breed. In fact, a recent Pug Dog Club of America health survey found that the number one response from owners was that their dog was healthy! And that's just how the PDCA wants to keep it.

asites, and properly nourished. For these reasons, a visit to the veterinarian who cared for the dam (mother) is recommended if at all possible. The dam passes disease resistance to her puppies, which should last from eight to ten weeks. Unfortunately, she can also pass on parasites and infection. This is why knowledge about her health is useful in learning more about the health of the puppies.

Now that you have your Pug puppy home safe and sound, it's time to arrange your

Choosing the right vet is the first step in raising a healthy puppy.

Dental health is vital to your puppy's overall well-being.

pup's first trip to the veterinarian. Perhaps the breeder can recommend someone in the area who specializes in Pugs, or maybe you know other Pug owners who can suggest a good vet. Either way, you should make an appointment within a couple of days of bringing home your puppy. If possible, see if you can stop for this first vet appointment before going home.

The pup's first vet visit will consist of an overall examination to make sure that the pup does not have any problems that are not apparent to you. The veterinarian also will set up a schedule for the pup's vaccinations; the breeder will inform you of which ones the dog has already received, and the vet can continue from there.

The puppy also will have his teeth examined and have his skeletal conformation and general health checked prior to certification by the veterinarian. Puppies in certain breeds have problems with their kneecaps,

NOTABLE & QUOTABLE

[Brachycephalic syndrome] patients typically make noise from the respiratory tract—snorting, snuffling, coughing, or gagging. In severe cases, dogs can experience episodes of difficulty breathing and exercise intolerance, with their gums and tongue turning blue to purple.

—Dr. Steven L. Marks, a diplomate of the American College of Veterinary Internal Medicine at North Carolina State University

cataracts and other eye problems, heart murmurs, and undescended testicles. They may also have personality problems, and your veterinarian might have training in temperament evaluation.

VACCINATION SCHEDULING

Most vaccinations are given by injection and should only be given by a veterinarian. Both you and the vet should keep a record of the date of the injection, the identification of the vaccine, and the amount given. Some vets give a first vaccination at eight weeks of age, but most dog breeders prefer the course not to commence until about ten weeks because of interaction with the antibodies produced by the mother. The vaccination scheduling is usually based on a fifteen-day cycle. You must take your vet's advice as to when to vaccinate, as this may differ according to the vaccine used.

The usual vaccines contain immunizing doses of several different viruses such as distemper, parvovirus, parainfluenza, and hepatitis. There are other vaccines available when the puppy is at risk. You should rely on your vet's advice. This is especially true for the booster immunizations. Most vaccination programs require a booster when the puppy is a year old and once a year thereafter. In some cases, circumstances may require more frequent immunizations.

Kennel cough, more formally known as tracheobronchitis, is immunized against with a vaccine that is sprayed into the dog's nostrils. Kennel cough is usually included in routine vaccinations, but it is often not as effective as the vaccines for other major diseases.

Your duty as a loving pet owner is to be on the lookout for any unusual signs or symptoms involving your dog's health.

Good physical health requires regular check-ups with the vet.

Your veterinarian probably will recommend that your Pug puppy be fully vaccinated before you take him on outings. There are airborne diseases, parasite eggs in the grass, and unexpected visits from other dogs that might be dangerous to your puppy's health. Other dogs are the most harmful reservoir of pathogenic organisms, as everything they have can be transmitted to your puppy.

Five Months to One Year of Age: Unless you intend to breed or show your dog, neutering/spaying your puppy at six months of age is recommended. Discuss this with your veterinarian. Neutering/spaying has proven to be beneficial to male and female puppies, respectively. Besides eliminating the possibility of pregnancy, it inhibits (but does not prevent) breast cancer in females and prostate cancer in male dogs.

Your veterinarian should provide your Pug puppy with a thorough dental evaluation at six months of age, ascertaining whether all his permanent teeth have erupted properly. A home dental care regimen should be initiated at six months, including brushing weekly and providing good dental devices (such as nylon bones). Regular dental care promotes healthy teeth, fresh breath, and a longer life.

Dogs Older Than One Year: Continue to visit the veterinarian at least once a year. There is no such disease as "old age," but bodily functions do change with age. The

Pugs have many physical quirks, so do your research and stay informed!

Heat stroke is a life-threatening emergency that can lead to multiple organ failure and death. If your dog does become overheated, it's critical that you cool him and transport him immediately to a veterinary facility. Apply cool—not cold—water or wet towels all over the dog's body. Transport him to the veterinary hospital with the windows open or the air conditioning on. Even if your dog starts to look better, he should still be examined.

—Dr. Steven L. Marks, a Diplomate of the American College of Veterinary Internal Medicine

eyes and ears are no longer as efficient. Liver, kidney, and intestinal functions often decline. Proper dietary changes, recommended by your veterinarian, can make life more pleasant for your aging Pug and you.

EVERYDAY HAPPENINGS

Keeping your Pug healthy is a matter of keen observation and quick action when necessary. Knowing what's normal for your dog will help you recognize signs of trouble before they blossom into a full-blown emergency situation.

Even if the problem is minor, such as a cut or scrape, you'll want to care for it immediately to prevent infection, as well as to ensure that your dog doesn't make it worse by chewing or scratching at it. Here's what to do for

Just like with infants, puppies need a series of vaccinations to ensure that they stay healthy during their first year of life. Download a vaccination chart from **DogChannel.com/Club-Pug** that you can fill out for your Pug.

common, minor injuries or illnesses, and how to recognize and deal with emergencies.

Cuts and Scrapes: For a cut or scrape that's half an inch or smaller, clean the wound with saline solution or warm water and use tweezers to remove any splinters or other debris. Apply antibiotic ointment. No bandage is necessary unless the wound is on a paw, which can pick up dirt when your dog walks on it. Deep cuts with lots of bleeding or those caused by glass or some other object should be treated by your veterinarian.

Cold Symptoms: Dogs don't actually get colds, but they can get illnesses that have similar symptoms, such as coughing, a runny nose, or sneezing. Dogs cough for any number of reasons, from respiratory infections to inhaled irritants to congestive heart failure. Take your Pug to the veterinarian for prolonged coughing, or coughing accompanied by labored breathing, runny eyes or nose, or bloody phlegm.

A runny nose that continues for more than several hours requires veterinary attention, as well. If your Pug sneezes, he may have some mild nasal irritation that will resolve on its own, but frequent sneezing, especially if it's accompanied by a runny nose, may indicate anything from allergies to an infection to something stuck in the nose.

Vomiting and Diarrhea: Sometimes dogs suffer minor gastric upsets when they eat a new type of food, eat too much, eat the contents of the trash can, or become excited or anxious. Give your Pug's stomach a rest by withholding food for twelve hours, and then feeding him a bland diet such as baby food or rice and chicken, gradually returning your Pug to his normal food. Projectile vomiting, or vomiting or diarrhea that continues for more than forty-eight hours, is another matter. If this happens, take your Pug to the veterinarian.

MORE HEALTH HINTS

A Pug's anal glands can cause problems if not evacuated periodically. In the wild, anal glands are cleared regularly to set the dog's mark, but in domestic dogs this function is no longer necessary; thus, their contents can build up and clog, causing discomfort. Signs that the anal glands on either side of the anus need emptying are if a Pug drags its rear end along the ground or keeps turning around to attend to the uncomfortable patch.

While care must be taken not to cause injury, anal glands can be evacuated by pressing gently on either side of the anal opening and by using a piece of cotton or a tissue to collect the foul-smelling matter. If anal glands are allowed to become impacted, abscesses can form, causing pain and the need for veterinary attention.

Pugs can get into all sorts of mischief, so it is not unknown for them to inadvertently swallow something poisonous in the course of their investigations. Obviously an urgent visit to your vet is required under such circumstances, but if possible, when you telephone him, you should advise which poisonous substance has been ingested, as different treatments are needed. Should it be necessary to cause your dog to vomit (which is not always the case with poisoning), a small lump of baking soda, given orally, will have an immediate effect. Alternatively, a small teaspoon of salt or mustard, dissolved in water, will have a similar effect but may be more difficult to administer and not as quick in its action.

Pug puppies often have painful fits while they are teething. These are not usually serious and are fleetingly brief, caused only by the pain of teething. Of course you must be certain that the cause is not more serious, but giving a puppy something hard on which to chew will usually solve this temporary problem.

BRACHYCEPHALIC SYNDROME

Pugs are a brachycephalic breed, meaning they have flat faces and short muzzles. As such, brachy dogs have the anatomical components of a regular size muzzle but in a much smaller, compressed space. The jaws develop normally in width but not in length, sometimes giving rise to anatomical and physiological problems collectively known as brachycephalic syndrome.

Brachycephalic syndrome manifests as airway interference and breathing disorders. Conditions relating to this syndrome include:

■ stenotic nares (narrowed or constricted nostril openings)

■ redundant pharyngeal tissue (folds of excess tissue in the throat)

■ everted laryngeal saccules (small structures on the side of the larynx are pulled out of position, into and blocking the opening into the lower airway)

■ elongated soft palate (the palate is too long in proportion to the head and it extends into the throat)

■ hypoplastic trachea (abnormal growth of the cartilage rings that comprise the trachea, resulting in a narrowed airway)

■ collapsed larynx (breakdown of the laryngeal walls)

■ heat and exercise intolerance (overheating resulting in respiratory stress)

OVEREXPOSURE

Like other brachycephalic dogs, Pugs are more prone to the perils of hyperthermia—another word for overheating. Hyperthermia is a dangerous condition that can cause seizures, brain and other internal damage, collapse, coma and death if not treated quickly enough.

To help avoid heat stress in your Pug, try the following techniques:

■ During hot, humid weather, keep your dog in air conditioning.

■ Make sure your Pug always has access to cool, shady areas and unlimited fresh water.

■ Avoid activities during the heat of the day; limit exercise and play times to early morning or late evening when it's cooler.

■ Monitor outside play and exercise so your dog doesn't overexert herself, reducing the length and intensity of exercise during hot spells.

■ Douse your Pug dog with a little cool water or wet towels when he's exercising, and wash his feet with cool water if he starts to get hot.

OF HEALTH

Full of charm and spunk, the rascally little Pug is a low-maintenance dog celebrated for his friendly temperament and good health; Pugs generally live to about twelve to fourteen years of age and seldom have the debilitating problems seen in some breeds. However, Pugs are not immune to genetic disease; like all creatures, defective genes can be passed along through the generations, sometimes resulting in genetic disease.

SKIN PROBLEMS

Veterinarians are consulted by dog owners for skin problems more than any other group of diseases or maladies. A dog's skin is as sensitive, if not more so, as human skin, and both suffer almost the same ailments (though the occurrence of acne in most breeds of dog is rare!). For this reason, veterinary dermatology has developed into a specialty practiced by many veterinarians.

Because many skin problems have visual symptoms that are almost identical, it requires the skill of an experienced veterinary dermatologist to identify and cure many of the more severe skin disorders. Pet-supply stores sell many treatments for skin problems, but most of them are directed at symptoms and not at the underlying problem(s). If your Pug puppy

Did You Know? **Dogs can get many diseases from ticks,** including Lyme disease, Rocky Mountain spotted fever, tick bite paralysis, and many others.

is suffering from a skin disorder, seek professional assistance as quickly as possible. As with all diseases, the earlier a problem is identified and treated, the more likely that the cure will be successful. There are active programs being undertaken by many veterinary pharmaceutical manufacturers to solve most, if not all, of the common skin problems in dogs.

SMART TIP! **Many skin irritations can be prevented or reduced by employing a simple preventive regimen:**

- Keep your Pug's skin folds clean and dry.
- Shampoo your dog regularly (particularly during the summer, which gives rise to many allergic conditions) with a hypoallergenic shampoo.
- Rinse the coat thoroughly.
- Practice good flea control.
- Supplement his diet with fatty acids.

PARASITE BITES

Insect bites itch, erupt, and may even become infected. Dogs have the same reaction to fleas, ticks, and/or mites. When an insect lands on you, you can whisk it away with your hand. Unfortunately, when a dog is bitten by a flea, tick, or mite, he can only scratch or bite. By the time your Pug has been bitten, the parasite has done its damage. It may also have laid eggs, which will cause further problems. The itching from parasite bites is probably due to the saliva injected into the site when the parasite sucks the dog's blood.

AIRBORNE ALLERGIES

Just as humans suffer from hay fever during the pollinating season, many dogs suffer from the same allergies. When the pollen count is high, your Pug might suffer, but don't expect him to sneeze or have a runny nose like a human. Dogs react to pollen allergies in the same way they react to fleas; they scratch and bite themselves. Dogs, like humans, can be tested for allergens. Discuss the testing with your vet.

AUTO-IMMUNE ILLNESS

An auto-immune illness is one in which the immune system overacts and does not recognize parts of the affected person. Instead, the immune system starts to react as if these parts were foreign and need to be destroyed. An example is rheumatoid arthritis, which occurs when the body does not recognize the joints, and this leads to a very painful and damaging reaction in the joints. This has nothing to do with age, so it can occur in puppies. The wear-and-tear arthritis in older people or dogs is called osteoarthritis.

Lupus is another auto-immune disease that affects dogs as well as people. It can take variable forms, affecting the kidneys, bones, and the skin. It can be fatal, so it is treated with steroids, which can themselves have very significant side effects. Steroids calm down the allergic reaction to the body's tissues, which helps the lupus, but also calms down the body's reaction to real foreign substances such as bacteria, and also thins the skin and bones.

FOOD ALLERGIES

Feeding your Pug properly is very important. An incorrect diet could affect your dog's health, behavior, and nervous system, possibly making a normal dog an aggressive one. The result of a good—or bad—diet is most visible in a dog's skin and coat, but internal organs are affected, too.

Dogs are allergic to many foods that are popular and highly recommended by breeders and veterinarians. Changing the brand of

Fleas are a common problem for all dog owners. Fight fleas by treating your dog's environment and your dog.

Did You Know? Across the globe, more than 800 species of ticks exist, and they aren't particular to where they dine. Mammals, birds, and reptiles are all fair game.

food may not eliminate the problem if the ingredient to which your dog is allergic is contained in the new brand.

Recognizing a food allergy can be difficult. Humans often have rashes or swelling of the lips or eyes when they eat foods they are allergic to. Dogs do not usually develop rashes, but they react the same way they do to an airborne or bite allergy—they itch, scratch, and bite. While pollen allergies and parasite bites are usually seasonal, food allergies are year-round problems.

Diagnosis of a food allergy is based on a two- to four-week dietary trial with a home-cooked diet fed to the exclusion of all other foods. The diet should consist of boiled rice or potato with a source of protein that your Pug has never eaten before, such as fresh or frozen fish, lamb, or even something as exotic as pheasant. Water has to be the only drink, and it is important that no other foods are fed during this trial. If your dog's condition improves, try the original diet again to see if the itching resumes. If it does, then your dog is allergic to his original diet. You must find a diet that does not distress your dog's skin. Start with a commercially available hypoallergenic diet or the homemade diet that you created for the allergy trial.

Food intolerance is the inability of the dog to completely digest certain foods. This occurs because the dog does not have the chemicals (enzymes) necessary to digest some foodstuffs. All puppies have the enzymes necessary to digest canine milk, but some dogs do not have the enzymes to digest cow milk, resulting in loose bowels, stomach pains, and the passage of gas.

Dogs often do not have the enzymes to digest soy or other beans. The treatment is to exclude these foods from your Pug's diet.

EXTERNAL PARASITES

Fleas: Of all the problems to which dogs are prone, none is better known and more frustrating than fleas. Flea infestation is relatively simple to cure but difficult to prevent.

To control flea infestation, you have to understand the flea's life cycle. Fleas are often thought of as a summertime problem, but centrally heated homes have made fleas a year-round problem. The most effective method of flea control is a two-stage approach: kill the adult fleas, then control the development of pre-adult fleas. Unfortunately, no single active ingredient is effective against all stages of the flea life cycle.

Treating fleas should be a two-pronged attack. First, the environment needs to be treated; this includes carpets and furniture, especially your Pug's bedding and areas underneath furniture. The environment should be treated with a household spray containing an insect growth regulator and an insecticide to kill the adult fleas. Most IGRs are effective against eggs and larvae; they actually mimic the fleas' own hormones and stop the eggs and larvae from developing into adult fleas. There are currently no treatments available to attack the pupae stage of the life cycle, so the adult insecticide is used to kill the newly hatched adult fleas before they find a host. Most IGRs are active for many months, while adult insecticides are only active for a few days.

When treating with a household spray, vacuum before applying the product. This stimulates as many pupae as possible to hatch into adult fleas. The vacuum cleaner should also be treated with an insecticide to prevent the eggs and larvae that have been collected in the vacuum bag from hatching.

The second stage of treatment is to apply an adult insecticide to your Pug. Traditionally, this would be in the form of a collar or a spray, but more recent innovations include digestible insecticides that poison the fleas when they ingest the dog's blood. Alternatively, there are drops that, when placed on the back of the dog's neck, spread throughout the hair and skin to kill adult fleas.

Ticks: Though not as common as fleas, ticks are found all over the tropical and temperate world. They don't bite like fleas; they harpoon. They dig their sharp proboscis (nose) into your Pug's skin and drink the blood, which is their only food and drink. Ticks are controlled the same way fleas are controlled.

The American dog tick, *Dermacentor variabilis*, may well be the most common dog tick in many geographical areas, especially those areas where the climate is hot and humid. Most dog ticks have life expectancies of a week to six months, depending on climatic conditions. They can neither jump nor fly, but they can crawl slowly and can range up to sixteen feet to reach a sleeping or unsuspecting dog.

Mites: Just as fleas and ticks can be problematic for your dog, mites can also lead to an itch fit. Microscopic in size, mites are related to ticks and generally take up permanent residence on their host animal—in this case, your Pug! The term "mange" refers to any infestation caused by one of the mighty mites, of which there are six varieties that smart dog owners should know.

● *Demodex mites* cause a condition known as demodicosis (sometimes called "red mange" or "follicular mange"), in which the mites live in the dog's hair follicles and sebaceous glands in larger-than-normal numbers. Most dogs recover from this type of mange without any treatment, though topical therapies are commonly prescribed by the vet.

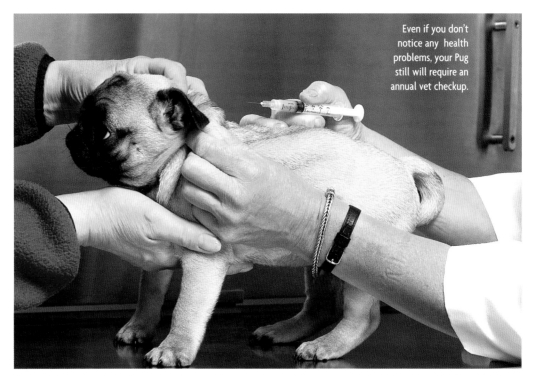

Even if you don't notice any health problems, your Pug still will require an annual vet checkup.

● The *Cheyletiellosis mite* is the hook-mouthed culprit associated with "walking dandruff," a condition that affects dogs as well as cats and rabbits. If untreated, this mange can affect a whole kennel of dogs and can be spread to humans, as well.

● The *Sarcoptes mite* causes intense itching on the dog in the form of a condition known as scabies or sarcoptic mange. Scabies is highly contagious and can be passed to humans. Sometimes an allergic reaction to the mite worsens the severe itching associated with sarcoptic mange.

● Ear mites, *Otodectes cynotis*, lead to otodectic mange, which commonly affects the outer ear canal of the dog, though other areas can be affected as well. Your vet can prescribe a treatment to flush out the ears and kill any eggs in the ears. A complete month of treatment is necessary to cure this mange.

● Two other mites, less common in dogs, include *Dermanyssus gallinae* (the "poultry"

or "red mite") and *Eutrombicula alfreddugesi* (the North American mite associated with trombiculidiasis or chigger infestation). The types of mange caused by both of these mites must be treated by vets.

INTERNAL PARASITES

Most animals—fish, birds, and mammals, including dogs and humans—have worms and other parasites that live inside their bodies. According to Dr. Herbert R. Axelrod, a fish pathologist, there are two kinds of parasites: dumb and smart. The smart parasites live in peaceful cooperation with their hosts (symbiosis), while the dumb parasites kill their hosts. Most worm infections are relatively easy to control. If they are not controlled, they weaken the host dog to the point that other medical problems occur, but they do not kill the host as dumb parasites would.

Roundworms: Roundworms that infect dogs live in the dog's intestines and shed eggs continually. It has been estimated that a dog produces about six or more ounces of feces every day. Each ounce averages hundreds of thousands of roundworm eggs. There are no known areas in which dogs roam that do not contain roundworm eggs. Because roundworms infect people, too, it is wise to have your dog regularly tested.

Roundworm infection can kill puppies and cause severe problems in adult dogs, as the hatched larvae travel to the lungs and trachea through the bloodstream. Cleanliness is the best preventive for roundworms. Always pick up after your dog and dispose of feces in appropriate receptacles.

Hookworms: Hookworms are dangerous to humans as well as to dogs and cats, and can be the cause of severe anemia due to iron deficiency. The worm uses its teeth to attach itself to the dog's intestines and changes the site of its attachment about six times per day. Each time the worm repositions itself, the dog loses blood and can become anemic.

Symptoms of hookworm infection include dark stools, weight loss, general weakness, pale coloration, and anemia, as well as possible skin problems. Fortunately, hookworms are easily purged with a number of medications that have proven effective. Discuss these with your veterinarian. Most heartworm preventives include a hookworm insecticide, as well.

Humans, can be infected by hookworms through exposure to contaminated feces. Because the worms cannot complete their life cycle on a human, the worms simply infest the skin and cause irritation. As a preventive, use disposable gloves or a "poop-scoop" to pick up your dog's droppings and prevent your dog (or neighborhood cats) from defecating in children's play areas.

Tapeworms: There are many species of tapeworm, all of which are carried by fleas!

Fleas are so small that your Pug could pass them onto your hands, your plate, or your food, making it possible for you to ingest a flea that is carrying tapeworm eggs. While tapeworm infection is not life-threatening in dogs (smart parasite!), it can be the cause of a very serious liver disease in humans.

Whipworms: In North America, whipworms are counted among the most common parasitic worms in dogs. Affected dogs may only experience upset tummies, colic, and diarrhea. These worms, however, can live for months or years in the dog, beginning their larval stage in the small intestine, spending their adult stage in the large intestine and finally passing infective eggs through the dog's feces. The only way to detect whipworms is through a fecal examination, though this is not always foolproof. Treatment for whipworms is tricky, due to the worms' unusual life cycle, and often dogs are reinfected due to exposure to infective eggs on the ground. Cleaning up droppings in your backyard as well as in public places is

it's a
Fact

absolutely essential for sanitation purposes and the health of your dog and others.

Threadworms: Though less common than roundworms, hookworms, and those previously mentioned parasites, threadworms concern dog owners in southwestern United States and the Gulf Coast area where the climate is hot and humid.

Living in the small intestine of the dog, this worm measures a mere two millimeters and is round in shape. Like the whipworm, the threadworm's life cycle is very complex, and the eggs and larvae are passed through the feces.

A deadly disease in humans, threadworms readily infect people, mostly through the handling of feces. Threadworms are most often seen in young puppies. The most common symptoms include bloody diarrhea and pneumonia. Sick puppies must be isolated and treated immediately; vets recommend a follow-up treatment one month later.

Heartworms: Heartworms are thin, extended worms up to twelve inches long, that live in a dog's heart and the major blood vessels surrounding it. Dogs may have up to 200 heartworms. Symptoms may be loss of energy, loss of appetite, coughing, the development of a pot belly, and anemia.

Heartworms are transmitted by mosquitoes, which drink the blood of infected dogs and take in larvae with the blood. The larvae, called *microfilariae*, develop within the body of the mosquito and are passed on to the next dog bitten after the larvae mature. It takes two to three weeks for the larvae to develop to the infective stage within the body of the mosquito. Dogs are usually treated at about six weeks of age and maintained on a prophylactic dose given monthly.

Blood testing for heartworms is not necessarily indicative of how seriously your dog is infected. Although this is a dangerous dis-

Pugs are a healthy breed, so most owners will not have to face many major medical issues.

ease, it is not easy for a dog to be infected. Discuss the various preventives with your vet, because there are many different types now available. Together you can decide on a safe course of prevention for your dog.

PUG HEALTH PROBLEMS

As with other toy breeds, luxated patellas are not uncommon in Pugs. Epilepsy is considered a problem, as are two eye diseases, keratoconjunctivitis sicca and pigmentary keratitis. Although hip dysplasia is quite common in the breed—Pugs are ranked the second-highest for hip dysplasia—most breeders and owners do not consider this a serious problem, because the disease usually does not affect the Pug very much. On other the hand, Pug Dog Encephalitis is a rare disease, but one of the top concerns of Pug breeders due to its deadliness.

Pug Dog Encephalitis: PDE is an inflammation of the brain and its meninges (the membranes covering the brain and spinal cord). The cause of this fairly rare disease is unknown, but the disease progresses rapidly, and the outcome is fatal.

How the disease is inherited is also unknown. PDE is recessive (because affected dogs have normal parents) and autosomal (occurs with equal frequency in males and females). PDE occurs most commonly in young adults, although Pugs as young as four months of age have been diagnosed with PDE. The first clue owners have that anything is amiss is when the dog starts having seizures. Presumptive diagnosis is based on clinical signs, although that is not conclusive because several disorders can cause seizures.

Eye Diseases: Keratoconjunctivitis sicca and pigmentary keratitis are two sometimes-related eye diseases that cause diminished sight or blindness. Both are common problems in Pugs and were identified as the number one health concern of Pug owners in a survey conducted by the Pug Dog Club of America. Hereditary aspects of these eye afflictions are unknown.

KCS, also known as "dry eye," refers to an inadequate production of tears. Tears are made of a mucous layer and a watery layer. With KCS, the eye stops making the watery layer. The cornea responds by thickening and turning leathery, and pigment is produced. Causes of KCS are many—congenital, autoimmune, viral, or a drug reaction. The nerves or tear glands may have failed or the ducts may be blocked.

Clinical signs of KCS include a dull, lackluster appearance to the eye and a thick, stringy discharge. As the disease worsens, the eye becomes infected, and the conjunctiva (mucous membrane covering the exposed portion of the eyeball and lining the inner surface of the eyelids) becomes red-

dened and inflamed. In most cases, the disease develops slowly; some owners may not even notice their dog is affected until their veterinarian spots telltale signs during a routine exam.

Pigmentary keratitis is an inflammatory condition of the cornea characterized by dark pigmentation spots that gradually spread across the surface of the eye. Seen more frequently in the bulgy-eyed breeds, PK can occur as a consequence of KCS (dry eye), entropion (inward rolling of the eyelids so that the hairs and lashes rub against the cornea), or environmental irritants (i.e., dust, wind). Clinical signs include dark pigments on the inside corner of the eyes.

Age of onset for KCS and PK is in young to middle-aged dogs. Treatment of the diseases consists of identifying and addressing any underlying problems, and then treating the clinical signs. Neither disease can be cured, but they can be arrested and some eyesight may be regained. In severely pigmented cases, a keratectomy (surgery that

peels off the pigmented layers of the eye) may be able to achieve partial to complete eyesight restoration.

You should have your Pugs' eyes tear-tested every year; a general veterinarian can do this. If the tear levels are dropping, [a veterinarian can] start therapy before the dog becomes totally affected. Also look closely at the dog's eyes. If you start seeing cloudy or dark pigments, take the dog to the veterinarian for a more thorough exam. The sooner treatment is introduced, the more eyesight the dog will retain.

Patellar Luxation: Patellar luxation (dislocated knee caps) is a common problem in many small and toy breeds, including the Pug. The patella is the flat, movable bone at the front of the knee; it slides up and down in a groove in the femur (the long upper bone of the hind leg or the human equivalent of the thigh bone) thus allowing the dog to bend or straighten his leg. The patellar ligament and the attached muscles maintain the patella in its position in this groove.

Sometimes, though, the groove is not deep enough, making it easier for the patella to shift out of place. In other cases, the muscles, tendons, ligaments or bones are misaligned, causing the patella to shift out of its path. Treatment is a surgical correction of the alignment and, if necessary, weight management to keep extra pounds from exacerbating the problem.

In the toy and small breeds, the most common type of patellar luxation is medial luxation, where the kneecap slips to the inside of the rear leg; this often occurs bilaterally (in both legs). Lateral luxation, in which the kneecap shifts toward the outside of the rear leg, generally occurs in large breeds.

The condition is thought to be a genetic and congenital disease. Although the deformities that cause luxations are present at birth, the dislocation could happen at any time during the dog's life—or never.

Clinical signs can be detected in toy breeds as young as five to eight weeks old, especially if there are severe deformities. Less commonly, some dogs don't show any signs of luxation until they are older: Tissues age, and the collagen and connecting tissues weaken, allowing the patella to luxate.

Diagnosis is based on physical exam and radiographs. Luxations are graded according to severity:

Because genetics is the biggest factor in patella problems, selecting away from lines that have increased incidence is probably the best way for breeders to help prevent the disease. Otherwise, an owner can do little to prevent patellar luxations from developing.

The Orthopedic Foundation for Animals maintains a registry for patellar luxations. The purpose is to identify dogs that are phenotypically normal (dogs in which the visible expression of the genetic trait appears normal) prior to breeding and to gather data on the disease.

Idiopathic Epilepsy: Idiopathic epilepsy is a disorder associated with recurrent seizures that are not a consequence of other disorders (i.e., head trauma, low blood sugar, poisoning, or kidney or liver failure). Affecting more than thirty-five different dog breeds, it is one of the most common diseases of the nervous system in dogs: a 1999 survey ranked idiopathic epilepsy as one of the top canine health issues identified by the American Kennel Club breed parent clubs.

Clinical signs may include uncontrolled jerking or rigidity of the entire body, head shaking, shivering, inability to stand, and strange behaviors, such as snapping at the air or foaming at the mouth. Because these clinical signs may also appear with other disorders, idiopathic epilepsy is difficult to

Research common Pug problems so you know in advance which issues may arise.

diagnose; the diagnosis is actually made by excluding other possible causes.

In most dogs, clinical signs of the disease can be managed or minimized, although not cured, by lifelong treatment with anticonvulsant drugs.

In the meantime, until markers and screening tests are identified for specific breeds, breeders should avoid breeding any dog with recurrent seizures for which idiopathic epilepsy has been diagnosed or is highly suspected and avoid a repeat breeding that previously produced offspring with epilepsy.

CHAPTER 8

A TOY DOG'S

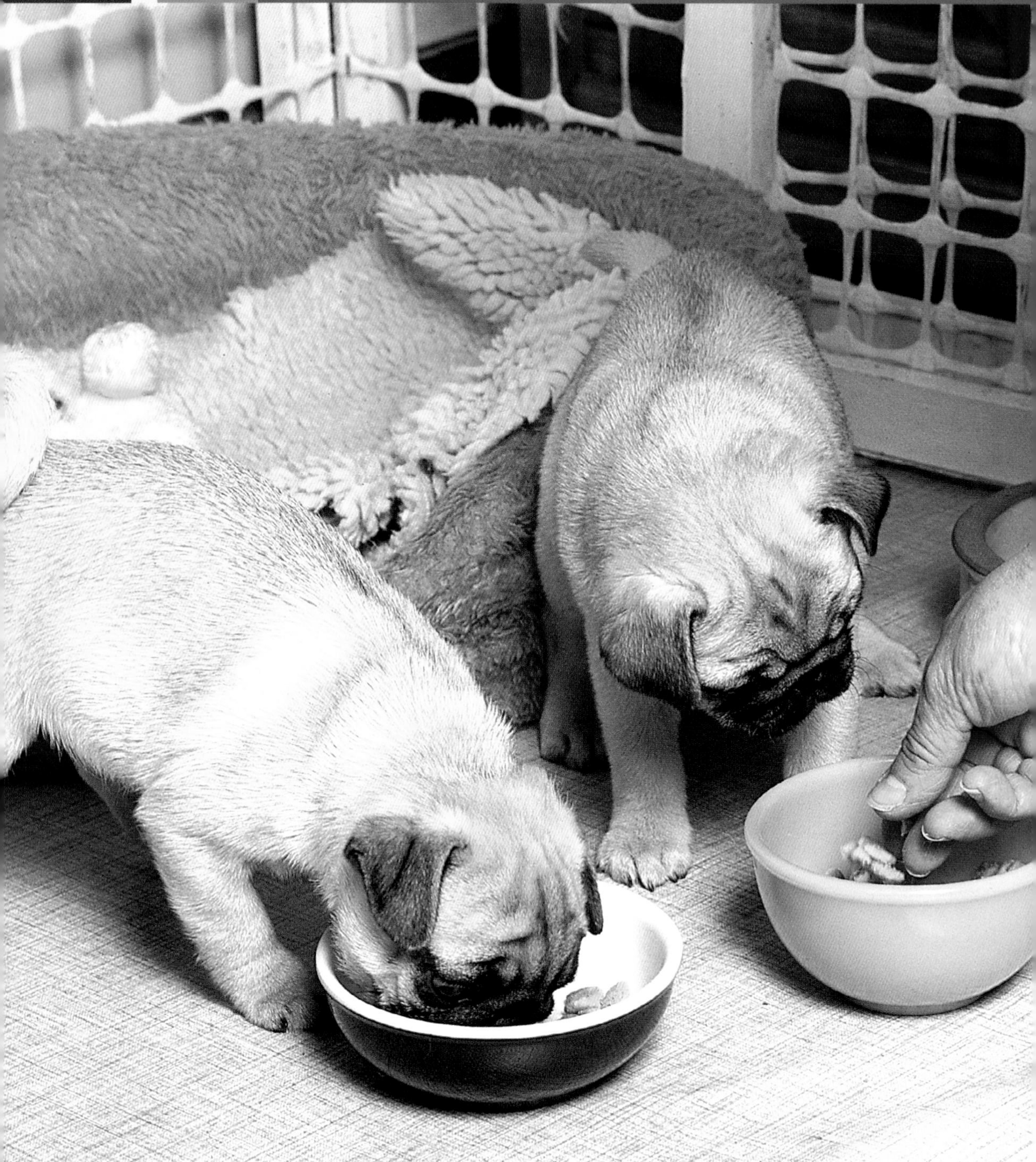

DINNER

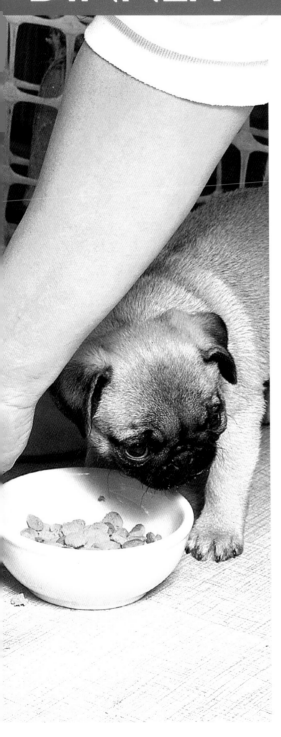

You have probably heard it a thousand times—you are what you eat. Believe it or not, it is very true. For dogs, they are what you feed them because they have little choice in the matter. Even smart owners who truly want to feed their dogs the best often cannot do so because they do not know which foods are best for their dogs.

Pugs can undoubtedly be greedy eaters, so it is important not to allow your dog to overeat. A Pug that is overweight has additional strain put on both the heart and on the joints, and any overweight dog is at greater risk under anesthesia. Also, old Pugs that are carrying too much weight can have great difficulty in using their back legs well, another reason why sensible dietary control is important.

BASIC TYPES

Dog foods are produced in various types: dry, wet (canned), semimoist, fresh packaged, and frozen.

Dry dog food is useful for the cost-conscious because it tends to be less expensive than the others. These foods also contain the least fat and the most preserva-

it's a Fact

Bones can cause gastro-intestinal obstruction and perforation, and may be contaminated with salmonella or E. coli. Leave them in the trash and give your dog a nylon bone toy instead.

tives. Dry food is bulky and takes longer to eat than other foods, so it's more filling.

Wet food—available in cans or foil pouches—is usually sixty to seventy percent water and is more expensive than dry food, but this isn't a major concern with small dogs such as Pugs. A palatable source of concentrated nutrition, wet food also makes a good supplement for underweight dogs or those recovering from illness. Some owners add a little wet food to dry food to increase its appeal, and dogs gobble up this mixture.

Semimoist food is flavorful but usually contains lots of sugar, which can lead to dental problems and obesity. It's not a good choice for your diminutive dog's main diet.

Likewise, **frozen** food, which is available in cooked and raw forms, is usually more expensive than wet foods. The advantages of frozen food are similar to those of wet foods.

Some manufacturers have developed special foods for small dogs. Some of these contain slightly more protein, fat, and calories than standard foods. Manufacturers contend that small dogs need these additional nutrients to fuel their active lifestyle and revved-up metabolism. In reality, your toy dog may or may not need them; the nutritional needs of dogs vary considerably, even within the same breed. It's OK to feed your Pug small-breed food, but know that standard food will provide balanced nutrition, too, as long as you feed appropriate amounts tailored to your buddy's needs.

Some dry foods for small dogs have compositions that are identical to those for larger dogs, but the kibble size is smaller to make it easier to chew. Small dogs don't really need smaller kibble, though your dog may prefer it. Many small dogs eat standard-size kibble with no trouble at all.

The amount of food your Pug needs depends on a number of factors, such as age, activity level, food quality, reproductive status, and size. What's the easiest way to figure it out? Start with the manufacturer's recommended amount, then adjust it according to your dog's response. For example, feed the recommended amount for a few weeks and if your Pug loses weight, increase the amount by ten to twenty percent. If your dog gains weight, decrease the amount. It won't take long to determine the amount of food that keeps your little friend in optimal condition.

Pugs love to eat and can become overweight, so limit your dog's daily food intake.

NUTRITION 101

All Pugs (and all dogs, for that matter) need proteins, carbohydrates, fats, vitamins, and minerals for their optimal growth and health.

■ **Proteins** are used for growth and repair of muscles, bones, and other bodily tissues. They're also used for production of antibodies, enzymes, and hormones. All dogs need protein, but it's especially important for puppies because they grow and develop so rapidly. Protein sources include various types of meat, meat meal, meat byproducts, eggs, dairy products, and soybeans.

■ **Carbohydrates** are metabolized into glucose, the body's principal energy source. Carbohydrates are available as sugars, starches, and fiber.

JOIN OUR ONLINE
Pug Club

Believe it or not, during your Pug's lifetime, you'll buy a few thousand pounds of dog food! Go to **DogChannel.com/Club-Pug** and download a chart that outlines the cost of dog food.

- Sugars (simple carbohydrates) are not suitable nutrient sources for dogs.
- Starches—a preferred type of carbohydrates in dog food—are found in a variety of plant products. Starches must be cooked in order to be digested.
- Fiber (cellulose)—also a preferred type of carbohydrate in dog food—isn't digestible but helps the digestive tract function properly.

■ **Fats** are also used for energy and play an important role in skin and coat health, hormone production, nervous system function, and vitamin transport. Fat increases the palatability and the calorie count of puppy/dog food, which can lead to serious health problems, such as obesity, for puppies or dogs that are allowed to overindulge. Some foods contain added amounts of omega fatty acids such as docosohexaenoic acid, a compound that may enhance brain development and learning in puppies but is not considered an essential nutrient by the Association of American Feed Control Officials (www.aafco.org). Fats used in dog foods include tallow, lard, poultry fat, fish oil and vegetable oils.

■ **Vitamins and minerals** help muscle and nerve functions, bone growth, healing, metabolism, and fluid balance. Especially important for your puppy are calcium, phosphorus, and vitamin D, which must be supplied in the right balance to ensure proper development of bones and teeth.

Don't just feed your Pug the cheapest brand of food you can find. Ask a vet for advice when planning your furry friend's diet.

Dogs of all ages love treats and table food, but these goodies can unbalance your Pug's diet and lead to a weight problem if you don't choose and feed them wisely. Table food, whether fed as a treat or as part of a meal, shouldn't account for more than ten percent of your Pug's daily caloric intake. If you plan to give your Pug treats, be sure to include "treat calories" when calculating the daily food requirement—so you don't end up with a pudgy pup!

When shopping for packaged treats, look for ones that provide complete nutrition—they're basically dog food in a fun form. Choose crunchy goodies for chewing fun and dental health. Other ideas for tasty treats include:

✓ small chunks of cooked, lean meat
✓ dry dog food morsels
✓ cheese
✓ veggies (cooked, raw or frozen)
✓ breads, crackers, or dry cereal
✓ unsalted, unbuttered, plain, popped popcorn

Some foods, however, can be dangerous and even deadly to a dog. The following items can cause digestive upset (vomiting or diarrhea) or toxic reactions that could be fatal:

✗ **avocados:** can cause gastrointestinal irritation, with vomiting and diarrhea, if eaten in sufficient quantity

✗ **baby food:** may contain onion powder; does not provide balanced nutrition

✗ **chocolate:** contains methylxanthines and theobromine, caffeine-like compounds that can cause vomiting, diarrhea, heart abnormalities, tremors, seizures, and death. Darker chocolates contain higher levels of the toxic compounds.

✗ **eggs, raw:** whites contain an enzyme that prevents uptake of biotin, a B vitamin; may contain salmonella

✗ **garlic (and related foods):** can cause gastrointestinal irritation and anemia if eaten in sufficient quantity

✗ **grapes:** can cause kidney failure if eaten in sufficient quantity (the toxic dose varies from dog to dog)

✗ **macadamia nuts:** can cause vomiting, weakness, lack of coordination, and other problems.

✗ **meat, raw:** may contain harmful bacteria such as salmonella or E. coli

✗ **milk:** can cause diarrhea in some puppies.

✗ **onions (and related foods):** can cause gastrointestinal irritation and anemia if eaten in sufficient quantity

✗ **raisins:** can cause kidney failure if eaten in sufficient quantity (the toxic dose varies from dog to dog)

✗ **yeast bread dough:** can rise in the gastrointestinal tract, causing obstruction; produces alcohol as it rises

Just as your Pug needs proper nutrition from his food, **water** is an essential "nutrient" as well. Water keeps the dog's body properly hydrated and promotes normal function of the body's systems.

During house-training, it is necessary to keep an eye on how much water your Pug is drinking, but once he is reliably trained, he should have access to clean, fresh water at all times, especially if you feed dry food. Make sure that your Pug's water bowl is clean, and change the water often.

CHECK OUT THE LABEL

To help you get a feel for what you are feeding your dog, start by taking a look at the label on the package or can. Look for the words "complete and balanced." This tells you that the food meets specific nutritional requirements set by the AAFCO for either adults ("maintenance") or puppies and pregnant/lactating females ("growth and reproduction"). The label must state the group for which it is intended. Because you're feeding a puppy, choose a "growth and reproduction" food.

The label also includes a nutritional analysis, which lists minimum protein, minimum fat, maximum fiber, and maximum moisture content, as well as other information. (You won't find carbohydrate content because it's everything that isn't protein, fat, fiber, and moisture.)

The nutritional analysis refers to crude protein and crude fat—amounts that have been determined in the laboratory. This analysis is technically accurate, but it doesn't tell you anything about digestibility: how much of the particular nutrient your Pug can actually use. For information about digestibility, contact the manufacturer (check the label for a telephone number and website address).

Virtually all commercial puppy foods exceed AAFCO's minimal requirements for protein and fat, the two nutrients most commonly evaluated when comparing foods. Protein levels in dry puppy foods usually range from about twenty-six to thirty percent; for canned foods, the values are about nine to thirteen percent. The fat content of dry puppy foods is about twenty percent or more; for canned foods, it's eight percent or more. (Dry food values are larger than canned food values because dry food contains less water; the values are actually similar when compared on a dry matter basis.)

Finally, check the ingredients on the label, which lists the ingredients in descending order by weight. Manufacturers are allowed to list separately different forms of a single ingredient (e.g., ground corn and corn gluten meal). The food may contain things like meat byproducts, meat and bone meal, and animal fat, which probably won't appeal to you but are nutritious and safe for your puppy. Higher quality foods usually have meat or meat products near the top of the ingredient list, but you don't need to worry about grain products as long as the label indicates that the food is nutritionally complete. Dogs are omnivores (not carnivores, as commonly

Feeding your dog is part of your daily routine. Take a break, and have some fun online and play "Feed the Pug," and exclusive game found only on **DogChannel.com/Club-Pug**—just click on "fun and games."

JOIN OUR ONLINE Pug Club

believed), so all balanced dog foods contain animal and plant ingredients.

STAGES OF LIFE

When selecting your dog's diet, three stages of development must be considered: the puppy stage, the adult stage, and the senior stage.

Puppy Diets: Pups instinctively want to nurse, and a normal puppy will exhibit this behavior from just a few moments following birth. Puppies should be allowed to nurse for about the first six weeks, although from the third or fourth week, the breeder will begin to introduce small portions of suitable solid food. Most breeders like to introduce alternate milk and meat meals initially, building up to weaning time.

By the time the puppies are seven or a maximum of eight weeks old, they should be fully weaned and fed solely on a proprietary puppy food. Selection of the most suitable, good-quality diet at this time is essential, for a puppy's fastest growth rate is during the first year of life. Seek advice about your dog's food from your veterinarian. The frequency of meals will be reduced over time, and when a young dog has reached the age of about ten to twelve months, he should be switched to an adult diet.

Did You Know?

If you're feeding a puppy food that's complete and balanced, your Pug youngster doesn't need any dietary supplements such as vitamins, minerals, or other types of food. Dietary supplementation could even harm your puppy by unbalancing his diet. If you have questions about supplementing your Pug's diet, ask your veterinarian.

How can you tell if your Pug is fit or fat? When you run your hands down your pal's sides from front to back, you should be able to easily feel his ribs. It's OK if you feel a little body fat (and, of course, a lot of hair), but you should not feel huge fat pads. You should also be able to feel your Pug's waist—an indentation behind the ribs.

Puppy and junior diets can be well balanced for the needs of your Pug so that, except in certain circumstances, additional vitamins, minerals, and proteins will not be required.

How many times a day does your Pug need to eat? Puppies—especially toy breeds—have small stomachs and high metabolic rates, so they need to eat several times a day in order to consume sufficient nutrients. If your puppy is younger than three months old, feed him four or five meals a day. When your little buddy is three to five months old, decrease the number of meals to three or four. At six months of age, most puppies can move to an adult schedule of two meals a day. If your Pug is prone to hypoglycemia (low blood sugar), a veterinarian may recommend more frequent meals.

Adult Diets: A dog is considered an adult when he has stopped growing. Rely on your veterinarian or dietary specialist to recommend an acceptable maintenance diet. Major dog food manufacturers specialize in this type of food, and smart owners must select the one best suited to their dogs' needs. Do not leave food out all day for "free-choice" feeding, as this freedom inevitably translates to inches around the dog's waist.

Senior Diets: As dogs get older, their metabolism changes. The older dog usually exercises less, moves more slowly, and sleeps more. This change in lifestyle and physiological performance requires a change in diet. Because these changes take place slowly, they might not be recognizable. These metabolic changes increase the tendency toward obesity, requiring an even more vigilant approach to feeding. Obesity in an older dog compounds the health problems that already accompany old age.

As your Pug gets older, few of his organs function up to par. The kidneys slow down,

Hypoglycemia (low blood sugar) is a potentially life-threatening problem for Pugs and other toy breeds. The most common type of hypoglycemia occurs in puppies younger than four months of age. Puppies typically develop hypoglycemia after exercising vigorously, when they're stressed (such as during a trip to the veterinarian) or when they've gone too long without eating.

Toy breed puppies have various anatomical, physiological, and behavioral factors that contribute to the development of hypoglycemia: small muscle mass and liver (areas where glucose is stored as glycogen, a large molecule made up of many molecules of glucose linked together), proportionately large brain (a major user of glucose), and high activity level. Immaturity of the body's systems for processing and storing glucose may also play a role.

Early symptoms—trembling, listlessness, incoordination, and a dazed or confused demeanor—occur when the brain is deprived of glucose, its sole energy supply. If untreated, hypoglycemia can lead to seizures, collapse, loss of consciousness, and death.

If your Pug develops symptoms of hypoglycemia, start treatment immediately. Wrap your little buddy in a towel or blanket to keep him warm (shivering makes the hypoglycemia worse). If your Pug is conscious, slowly dribble a little corn syrup or honey into his mouth or give him a dollop of high-calorie dietary-supplement paste (available from your veterinarian). Repeat after ten minutes, if necessary.

Feed your Pug puppy as soon as he's alert enough to eat. If hypoglycemia causes your Pug to lose consciousness, rub the syrup or paste on his gums and tongue, then immediately take your pal to the veterinarian for further care.

If your puppy is prone to developing hypoglycemia, you should feed him a high-quality nutritionally balanced food four to five times a day.

Healthy high-calorie snacks may help prevent hypoglycemia between meals. If possible, avoid subjecting your Pug puppy to circumstances that may elicit hypoglycemia, such as stressful situations or extended periods of vigorous activity. Most puppies outgrow hypoglycemia by the time they're four months old. Consult your veterinarian if your Pug continues to have hypoglycemic episodes after this age.

HYPOGLYCEMIA HELP

and the intestines become less efficient. These age-related factors are best handled with a change in diet and a change in feeding schedule to give smaller portions that are more easily digested.

There is no single best diet for every older dog. While many older dogs will do perfectly fine on light or senior diets, other dogs will do better on special premium diets such as lamb and rice. Be sensitive to your senior Pug's diet, and this will help control other problems that may arise with your old friend.

Did You Know?

Because semimoist food contains lots of sugar, it isn't a good selection for your Pug's main menu. However, it is great for an occasional yummy snack. Try forming into little meatballs for a once-a-week treat! He'll love ya for it!

These delicious, dog-friendly recipes will have your furry friend smacking his lips and salivating for more. Just remember: Treats aren't meant to replace your dog's regular meals. Give your Pug snacks sparingly and continue to feed him nutritious, well-balanced meals.

Cheddar Squares

$1/3$ cup all-natural applesauce
$1/3$ cup low-fat cheddar cheese, shredded
$1/3$ cup water
2 cups unbleached white flour

In a medium bowl, mix all wet ingredients. In a large bowl, mix all dry ingredients. Slowly add the wet ingredients to the dry mixture. Mix well. Pour batter into a greased 13x9x2-inch pan. Bake at 375-degrees Fahrenheit for 25 to 30 minutes. Bars are done when a toothpick inserted in the center and removed comes out clean. Cool and cut into bars. Makes about 54 one-and-a-half-inch bars.

Peanut Butter Bites

3 tablespoons vegetable oil
$1/4$ cup smooth peanut butter, no salt or sugar
$1/4$ cup honey
$1 1/2$ teaspoon baking powder
2 eggs
2 cups whole wheat flower

In a large bowl, mix all ingredients until dough is firm. If the dough is too sticky, mix in a small amount of flour. Knead dough on a lightly floured surface until firm. Roll out dough half an inch thick and cut with cookie cutters. Put cookies on a cookie sheet half an inch apart. Bake at 350-degrees Fahrenheit for 20 to 25 minutes. When done, cookies should be firm to the touch. Turn oven off and leave cookies for one to two hours to harden. Makes about 40 two-inch-long cookies.

LOOKING TOY

Pugs are dogs you can trust. The expression in their eyes and wrinkle brows seem to tell everyone that they care, they really care, about whatever concerns you at that moment. They are the empathetic breed of the dog world. Small, short-coated, and seemingly eager to please, a Pug worms his way into your heart and, before you know it, right into your home and family.

What could be easier to care for than a dog with extremely short, straight hair? How hard can it be? Hold it right there, partner. Looks can be deceiving.

Every breed has its challenges and Pugs are no different. Yes, they have short hair, but they also have protruding eyes, short noses, and wrinkles, oh, those wrinkles. It's true that grooming a Pug is easier and faster than, say, grooming an Afghan or a Shih Tzu. But before you click your heels and zoom out of the pet-supply store with only a bag of food, a couple of bowls, and the requisite collar and leash, take some time to investigate the breed you have just fallen in love with.

Did You Know? Nail clipping can be tricky, so many dog owners leave the task for the professionals. However, if you walk you dog on concrete, you may not have to worry about it. The concrete acts like a nail file and will probably keep the nails in check.

GEAR UP

No matter what the television commercial models with long, flowing tresses tell you, the ingredients you add externally to your pet's hair will not change a brittle, lifeless coat into a soft, healthy hair. The truth is that if you want your Pug to have a healthy coat, then take a close look at your dog's nutrition. Healthy hair and skin begins with good nutrition. A good premium dog food is the best place to start growing a healthy coat. Your pet's diet is not the place to economize. Purchase the best food you can afford, and resist the impulse to save money at your dog's expense. Pugs' skin can be sensitive, so consult your veterinarian when choosing your Pug's diet. Once you've established a good nutritional basis, you can move on to improving the coat from the outside.

In order to keep your Pug polished, you will need a few grooming essentials:

- a pair of nail clippers
- styptic powder
- cotton balls
- ear powder or cleaner
- tearless pet shampoo
- a coat conditioner
- hydrogen peroxide or a package of baby wipes
- a soft bristle or slicker brush

Although you won't need to worry about dematting your Pug, don't be too smug about your short-coated breed. Yes, even short hairs sheds, and if you thought it was safe to wear your navy blazer into the house in the middle of summer, think again. Pugs will shed short, prickly hair all over the house if you don't take the time to

Pugs require more grooming than you might think.

After removing a tick, clean the dog's skin with hydrogen peroxide. If Lyme disease is common where you live, have your veterinarian test the tick. Tick preventative medication will discourage ticks from attaching and kill any that do.

—groomer Andrea Vilardi from West Paterson, N.J.

brush your pet regularly. You're thinking: It's short, how bad can it be? Well, believe it or not, it can be bad. So, let's hear the pledge: On my honor, I promise to brush my Pug every other day in the summer. (Failing that, at the very least once a week, and I agree not to blame my Pug if I forget and end up looking like an escapee from a lint factory.)

BATHING BASICS

The key to a successful bath is organization. Keep all your grooming tools in a basket so you can set up for the bath in only a moment. (This comes in handy when your zestful Pug finds something interesting in the yard to roll in and you need to move quickly!)

You might consider a restraining device, which is available in pet-supply stores. One style has a suction cup that attaches to the side of the tub or sink, and a loop that slides over the head and one front leg. The dog is controlled, and the loop is not in danger of choking your dog's slender neck.

Check the temperature of the water against the inside of your wrist or with your hand. Hold the hose close to your dog's body to eliminate excessive spray. If you don't have a hose attachment, use a plastic cup to scoop water and pour it over the dog.

Pugs have shallow eye sockets. Trying to control movements by holding the crown of the head or any of those wrinkles can damage his eyes. Instead, place your hand under the chin and on the chest if you need to contain his activity.

—Susan Sholar, grooming salon owner/operator in San Marcos, Calif.

Work from the highest point to the lowest on the dog with the water and shampoo; use your fingers to work the shampoo throughout the coat. For the face, use a child's soft toothbrush to clean the mustache and around the eye area and beard. The bristles are soft, but stiff enough to distribute the shampoo.

JOIN OUR ONLINE
Pug Club

Every Pug should look dapper. What do you need to keep your pup looking his best? Go to Club Pug (**DogChannel.com/Club-Pug**) and download a checklist of essential grooming equipment you and your Pug will need.

To keep water from getting into the nose when you rinse this area, hold your hand as a barrier around the nose, and let the water flow from behind the ears toward your hand and sort of break against the hand, descending over the beard.

Rinse the dog with a gentle flow of water until the hair feels clean and the water runs clear. Use coat conditioners after a bath, but use sparingly so as not to clog the pores. Follow the instructions on the bottle.

DRY THAT PUG

When you are sure your Pug is completely rinsed, wrap him in a big, fluffy towel and dry, dry, dry. Don't allow your dog to jump from the bathtub. Wet paws and ceramic tile equals an ice rink for dogs—and broken bones. You don't want to be sitting around the fireplace twenty years from now and hear your grown children discussing the day 'Mom broke Buster's leg.' Continue drying the coat until you can feel most of the moisture has been removed. Then you can either allow your Pug to air dry (in the summer) or use a hand dryer to finish drying it.

Many pet-supply shops carry hair dryers specifically manufactured for pets. You also can use your own dryer. A word of caution: Your own dryer can generate heat too intense for your Pug. Turn it on a medium setting and test the temperature of the air-flow against the inside of your wrist. If it is uncomfortable to you then it is too hot for your Pug. Keep the setting low; even cool air will dry the coat. Never put your Pug in a cage and let a dryer run on it. This breed can overheat in an extremely short amount of time. If you use a grooming facility, insist that they either hand dry or air-dry your pet.

One more eye warning: Do not blow the air directly into your Pug's eyes. Breeds with large, bulging eyes, such as Pugs, require

SMART TIP!

The family pet shouldn't be the center of a power struggle between children and parents. Divvy up grooming and bathing responsibilities early on, and make the issue non-negotiable. A clean Pug is a pet that is welcomed into the house with the family; a dirty one is banished to the backyard, doomed to be on the outside looking in. Even short-coated breeds such as Pugs need a regular grooming routine.

that you stay aware of their eyes whenever you are grooming them.

PUG PEDICURES

Immediately after the bath is the best time to clip your dog's nails because the water has softened the nails, and your Pug may be somewhat tired-out by the bath. In fact, hope and pray that he is tired out from his bath, because, in general, Pugs hate to have their nails clipped. This may sound like a stereotype, but nine out of ten groomers will attest to the truthfulness of this statement.

You should trim your Pug's nails every two to three weeks. Periodic nail trimming can be done during the brushing routine. Your veterinarian will teach you how to cut your dog's nails without cutting the "quick" (the blood vessels that run through the center of each nail and grow rather close to the end).

Your Pug should be accustomed to having his nails trimmed at an early age because it will be part of your maintenance routine throughout his life. Not only does it look nicer, but long nails can scratch someone unintentionally. Also, a long nail has a better chance of ripping and bleeding, or causing the feet to spread. A good rule of thumb is that if you can hear your dog's nails' clicking on the floor when he walks, his nails are too long.

Before you start cutting, make sure you can identify the "quick" in each nail. It will bleed if accidentally cut, which will be quite painful for the dog because it contains nerve endings. Keep some type of clotting agent on hand, such as a styptic pencil or styptic powder (the type used for shaving). This will stop the bleeding quickly when applied to the end of the cut nail. Do not panic if you cut the quick. Just stop the bleeding and talk soothingly to your dog. Once he has calmed down, move on to the next nail. It is better to clip a little at a time, particularly with black-nailed dogs.

Hold your pup steady as you begin trimming his nails; you do not want him to make any sudden movements or run away. Talk to him soothingly and stroke him as you clip. Holding his foot in your hand, simply take off the end of each nail in one quick clip. You can purchase nail clippers that are specially

Pugs have very sensitive skin, so be gentle when grooming your little friend.

made for dogs; you can probably find them wherever you buy grooming supplies.

There are two predominant types of clippers. One is the guillotine clipper, which is a hole with a blade in the middle. Squeeze the handles, and the blade meets the nail and chops it off. Sounds gruesome, and for some dogs, it is intolerable. Scissor-type clippers are gentler on the nail. The important thing to make sure of is that the blades on either of these clippers are sharp. Once you are at the desired length, use a nail file to smooth the rough edges of the nails so they don't catch on carpeting or debris outdoors.

If the procedure becomes more than you can deal with, just remember: Groomers and veterinarians charge a nominal fee to clip nails. By using their services you won't have to see your pet glower at you for the rest of the night.

When inspecting feet, you must check not only the nails but also the pads of the feet. Take care that the pads have not become cracked and always check between the pads to be sure that nothing has become lodged there. Depending upon the season, there may be a danger of grass seeds or thorns becoming embedded, or even tar from the road getting stuck. Butter, by the way, is useful to help remove tar from his feet.

BRUSHING

Sit your dog in your lap or on a table or elevated surface. You can use a soft bristle brush, a soft slicker brush or a rubber curry brush to remove your Pug's shedding coat. Begin at the top of the neck and brush backward to its cute little curled tail. Then brush down the sides and under the chest. A few minutes a day will ensure that the dead hair is removed, and you can lead a relatively shed-free existence.

Forget to brush however, and don't be surprised if even strangers strike up a conversation about your pet because you will be wearing the evidence on your clothing. Those short, beige or black hairs cling to everything.

THE IMPORTANCE OF CLEAN TEETH

Like people, Pugs can suffer from dental disease, so experts recommend regular tooth brushing. Daily brushing is best, but your dog will benefit from tooth brushing a few times a week. The teeth should be white and free of yellowish tartar, and the gums should appear healthy and pink. Gums that bleed easily when you perform dental duties may have gingivitis.

The first thing to know is that your puppy probably isn't going to want your fingers in his mouth. Desensitizing your puppy—getting him to accept that you will be looking at and touching his teeth—is the first step to overcoming his reticence. You can begin this as soon as you get your puppy, with the help of the thing that motivates him most: food.

For starters, let your puppy lick some chicken, vegetable, or beef broth off your finger. Then, dip your finger in broth again, and gently insert your finger in the side of your dog's mouth. Touch his side teeth and gums. Several sessions will get your puppy used to having his mouth touched.

Use a toothbrush specifically made for a dog or a finger-tip brush wrapped around your finger to brush your Pug's teeth. Hold the mouth with the fingers of one hand, and

Did You Know? The crunchiness of unmoistened dry dog food helps keep teeth healthy by reducing plaque accumulation and massaging the gums.

brush with the other. Use toothpaste made specifically for dogs with dog-slurping flavors like poultry and beef. The human kind froths too much and can give your dog an upset stomach if swallowed. Brush in a circular motion with the brush held at a forty-five-degree angle to the gum line. Be sure to get the fronts, tops, and sides of each tooth.

Look for signs of plaque, tartar, or gum disease, including redness, swelling, foul breath, discolored enamel near the gum line, and receding gums. If you see these, take your dog to the veterinarian immediately. Also see your vet about once a year for a dental checkup.

HEAD, EYES, AND EARS

The wrinkles over the nose must never be allowed to get so dirty that sores develop, so at the very first sign that something is not as it should be, the area should be carefully wiped clean and smeared with pure lanolin or petroleum jelly. Some owners prefer to use Hibiscrub, an antimicrobial preparation used for pre-surgery hand disinfection; this also helps clear any infection. Black Pugs are rather prone to having their wrinkles become over-greasy, so this will also need to be checked. While considering this aspect of the Pug's face, it is also important never to let the nose itself become too dry, as this can sometimes happen in the breed.

Eyes and ears should also be carefully wiped clean. If necessary, use one of the proprietary cleansers available from pet-supply shops and other canine outlets. Make sure that a separate cotton ball or tissue is used for each eye and ear, so that there is no transfer of infection. Always check for any build-up of wax in the ear. This seems to occur with greater frequency in black Pugs. If caught early enough, a waxy build-up within the ear should be easy enough to

Keep your Pug's mouth clean to minimize the health problems that arise from bad dental hygiene.

cleanse, but never probe into the ear, as doing so can cause injury within the canal.

Be on the lookout for any signs of infection or ear-mite infestation. If your Pug has been shaking his head or scratching at his ears, this usually indicates a problem. If your dog's ears have an unusual odor, this is a sure sign of mite infestation or infection, and a signal to have his ears checked by the veterinarian.

While you're in the process of washing your Pug, gently wipe the inside of the ears with a damp face cloth. The ears should be kept clean and any excess hair inside the ear should be carefully plucked out. Take a commercial ear cleaner and place a few drops in each ear canal. Most dogs shake their heads when you do this. Have a towel handy to block the escaping solution. Never force your finger or any object down into the deeper part of the ear. Wipe only the surface you can see and touch easily. Any further cleaning must be performed by your vet.

REWARD A JOB WELL DONE

Rewarding your pet for behaving during grooming is the best way to ensure stress-free grooming throughout his lifetime. Bathing energizes your pet, and using the time immediately after grooming as play time is the best way to reward your Pug for a job well done. Watching your clean, healthy Pug tear from room to room in sheer joy is your reward for being a caring and smart owner.

If you are unwilling to groom your Pug yourself, ask your vet to recommend a professional groomer in your area.

Six Tips for Pug Care

1. Pugs have extremely sensitive eyes. Use only tearless shampoos and avoid getting shampoo in your Pug's eyes. At the first sign of irritation or clouding in the eyes see your veterinarian immediately.
2. Keep the folds and wrinkles around his face and nose scrupulously clean and dry. Use either a cotton ball dampened with a mild hydrogen peroxide solution, baby wipes, or a damp sponge. Wipe out the wrinkles daily and dry completely.
3. Using powder in the folds can cake and irritate the skin; it's better just to clean and dry the wrinkles, paying attention to the appearance of the skin.
4. Invest in a rubber curry brush. It will quickly pull any loose hairs out to prevent shedding. During shedding season, try to spend a few minutes every other day brushing your Pug.
5. Proper nail care helps with your dog's gait and spinal alignment. Nails that are too long can force a dog to walk improperly. Also, too-long nails can snag and tear, causing painful injury to your Pug.
6. Good dental health prevents gum disease and early tooth loss. Brush your Pug's teeth daily and see a veterinarian yearly.

Six Questions to Ask a Groomer

1. Do you cage dry? Are you willing to hand dry or air dry my pet?
2. What type of shampoo are you using? Is it tearless? If not, do you have a tearless variety available for use?
3. Will you restrain my pet if he acts up for nail-clipping? What methods do you use for difficult dogs?
4. Are you familiar with the breed? Do you have any references from other Pug owners?
5. Is the shop air-conditioned in hot weather?
6. Will my dog be getting brushed or just bathed? Will his wrinkles be cleaned and dried?

TIME TO

TRAIN

Pugs are intelligent, clever and eager to please, but even so, they don't always choose to obey. The reason for this is obvious: Pugs simply don't care to be told what to do. Pugs prefer to be invited. Pugs are sensitive sweethearts, but can be headstrong and sometimes teasingly naughty.

Yet these funny little fellows often earn the title "class clown" at obedience school because of their talent for finding playful alternatives for performing required exercises—or not. Smart owners know that the key to training Pugs lies in making education fun. And with positive techniques, such as lure-and-reward and clicker training, you can shape that little clown of yours into class valedictorian.

It's easy to fall into the trap of thinking your Pug doesn't need training. He's so little, it's no big deal to pick him up when you need to take him somewhere. But if you want him to be a mentally and physically healthy, well-adjusted member of society instead of a snappy little arm-shark, some basic training is in order. Whatever your goals for your relationship with your pint-sized pal, they'll be best achieved if you take the time to teach your Pug a solid foundation of good manners.

Did You Know?

The prime period for socialization is short. Most behavior experts agree that positive experiences during the ten-week period between four and fourteen weeks of age are vital to the development of a puppy who'll grow into an adult dog with sound temperament.

Reward-based training methods—clicker and luring—show dogs what to do and help them do it correctly, setting them up for success and rewards rather than mistakes and punishment. Most dogs find food rewards meaningful; Pugs are no exception. They tend to be very food-motivated. This works well because positive training relies on using treats, at least initially, to encourage the dog to demonstrate a behavior. The treat is then given as a reward. When you reinforce desired behaviors with rewards that are valuable to the dog, you are met with happy cooperation rather than resistance.

Positive reinforcement does not mean permissive. While you are rewarding your Pug's desirable behaviors, you must manage him to be sure he doesn't get rewarded for his undesirable behaviors. Training tools, such as leashes, tethers, baby gates, and crates, help keep your dog out of trouble, and the use of force-free negative punishment (the dog's behavior makes a good thing go away) helps him realize there are negative consequences for inappropriate behaviors.

Reward your Pug when he learns a new skill, and he will remember this behavior in the future.

LEARNING SOCIAL GRACES

Now that you have done all of the preparatory work and have helped your Pug get accustomed to his new home and family, it is time for you to have some fun! Socializing your tiny pup gives you the opportunity to show off your new friend, and your Pug gets to reap the benefits of being an adorable little creature that people will want to pet and, in general, think is absolutely precious!

Besides getting to know his new family, your puppy should be exposed to other people, animals, and situations, but, of course, he must not come into close contact with dogs who you don't know well until he has had all his vaccinations. This will help him become well adjusted as he grows up and less prone to being timid or fearful of the new things he will encounter.

Your pup's socialization began at the breeder's home, but now it is your responsibility to continue it. The socialization he receives up until the age of twelve weeks is the most critical, as this is the time when he forms his impressions of the outside world. Be especially careful during the eight- to ten-week period, also known as the fear period. The interaction he receives during this time should be gentle and reassuring. Lack of socialization can manifest itself in fear and aggression as the dog grows up. The pup needs lots of human contact, affection, handling, and exposure to other animals.

Once your Pug has received his necessary vaccinations, feel free to take him out and about (on his leash, of course). Walk him around the neighborhood, take him on your daily errands, let people pet him, let him meet other dogs and pets. Make sure to expose your Pug to different people—men, women, kids, babies, men with beards, teenagers with cell phones or riding skate-

SMART TIP!

If your Pug refuses to sit with both haunches squarely beneath him and instead sits on one side or the other, he may have a physical reason for doing so. Discuss the habit with your veterinarian to be certain that your dog isn't suffering from some structural problem.

boards, joggers, shoppers, someone in a wheelchair, a pregnant woman, etc. Make sure your Pug explores different surfaces like sidewalks, gravel, and a puddle. Positive experience is the key to building confidence. It's up to you to make sure your Pug safely discovers the world so he will be a calm, confident, and well-socialized dog.

It's important that you take the lead in all socialization experiences and never put your

Decide in advance whether you want your Pug to potty indoors or out, and stick to one place.

pup in a scary or potentially harmful situation. Be mindful of your Pug's limitations. Fifteen minutes at a public market is fine; two hours at a loud outdoor concert is too much. Meeting vaccinated, tolerant and gentle older dogs is great. Meeting dogs that you don't know isn't a great idea, especially if they appear very energetic, dominant, or fearful. Control the situations in which you place your pup.

The best way to socialize your puppy to a new experience is to make him think it's the best thing ever. You can do this with a lot of happy talk, enthusiasm, and, yes, food. To convince your puppy that almost any experience is a blast, always carry treats. Consider carrying two types—a bag of his puppy chow, which you can give him when introducing him to nonthreatening experiences, and a bag of high-value, mouth-watering treats to give him when introducing him to scarier experiences.

BASIC CUES

All Pugs, regardless of your training and relationship goals, need to know at least five basic good-manner behaviors: sit, down, stay, come, and heel. Here are tips for teaching your dog these important cues.

Sit: Every dog should learn how to sit.

▲ Hold a treat at the end of your Pug's nose.

▲ Move the treat over his head.

▲ When he sits, click a clicker or say "Yes!"

▲ Feed your dog the treat.

▲ If your dog jumps up, hold the treat lower. If he backs up, back him into a corner

Do not take your Pug on a walk before teaching him a new skill. An overly tired puppy will not learn as easily.

and wait until he sits. Be patient. Keep your clicker handy, and click (or say "Yes!") and treat anytime he offers a sit.

▲ When he easily offers sits, say "sit" just before he offers, so he can make the association between the word and the behavior. Add the sit cue when you know you can get the behavior. Your dog doesn't know what the word means until you repeatedly associate it with the appropriate behavior.

▲ When your Pug sits easily on cue, start using intermittent reinforcement by clicking some sits but not others. At first, click most sits and skip an occasional one (this is a high rate of reinforcement). Gradually make your clicks more and more random.

Down: If your Pug can sit, then he can learn to lie down.

▼ Have your Pug sit.

▼ Hold the treat in front of his nose. Move it down slowly, straight toward the floor (toward his toes). If he follows all the way down, click and treat.

▼ If he gets stuck, move the treat down more slowly. Click and treat for small movements downward—moving his head a bit lower, or inching one paw forward. Keep clicking and treating until your Pug is all the way down. This is called "shaping"—rewarding small pieces of a behavior until your dog succeeds.

▼ If your dog stands as you move the treat toward the floor, have him sit, and move the treat more slowly downward, shaping with clicks and treats for small movement down as long as he is sitting. If he stands, cheerfully

All dogs should learn the basics: sit, down, and come.

say "Oops!" (which means "Sorry, no treat for that!"), have him sit, and try again.

▼ If shaping isn't working, sit on the floor with your knee raised. Have your Pug sit next to you. Put your hand with the treat under your knee and lure him under your leg so that he lies down and crawls to follow the treat. Click and treat!

▼ When you can lure the down easily, add the verbal cue, wait a few seconds to let your dog think, then lure him down to show him the association. Repeat until he'll go down on the verbal cue. Then begin using intermittent reinforcement.

Stay: What good are sit and down cues if your dog doesn't stay?

In addition to treats, your Pug's favorite toy will make a great training aid.

● Start with your Pug in a sit or down position.

● Put the treat in front of your dog's nose and keep it there.

● Click and reward several times while he is in position, then release him with a cue that you will always use to tell him the stay is over. Common release cues are: "all done," "break," "free," "free dog," "at ease," and "OK."

Behaviors are best trained by breaking them down into their simplest components, teaching those, and then linking them together to end up with the complete behavior. Keep treats small so you can reward many times without stuffing your Pug. Remember, don't bore your Pug—avoid excessive repetition.

● When your Pug will stay in a sit or down position while you click and treat, add your verbal stay cue. Say "stay," pause for a second or two, click and say "stay" again. Release.

● When he's getting the idea, say "stay," whisk the treat out of sight behind your back, click, and whisk the treat back. Be sure to get it all the way to his nose, so he doesn't jump up. Gradually increase the duration of the stay.

● When your Pug will stay for fifteen to twenty seconds, add small distractions: shuffling your feet, moving your arms, small hops. Increase distractions gradually. If he makes mistakes, you're adding too much, too fast.

● When he'll stay for fifteen to twenty seconds with distractions, gradually add distance. Have your dog stay, take a half-step back, click, return, and treat. When he'll stay with a half-step, tell him to stay, take a full step back, click, and return. Always return to your dog to treat after you click, but before you release. If you always return, his stay becomes strong. If you call him to you, his stay gets weaker due to his eagerness to come to you.

Come: A reliable recall—coming when called—can be a challenging behavior to teach. It is possible, however. To succeed, you need to install an automatic response to your "come" cue—one so automatic that your Pug doesn't even stop to think when he hears it, but will spin on his heels and charge to you at full speed.

▓ Start by charging a come cue the same way you charged your clicker. If your Pug already ignores the word "come," pick a different cue, like "front" or "hugs." Say your cue and feed him a bit of scrumptious treat. Repeat this until his eyes light up when he hears the cue. Now you're ready to start training.

▓ With your Pug on a leash, run away several steps and cheerfully call out your

SMART TIP!

If you begin teaching the heel cue by taking long walks and letting the dog pull you along, he may misinterpret this action as an acceptable form of taking a walk. When you pull back on the leash to counteract his pulling, he will read that tug as a signal to pull even harder!

charged cue. When he follows, click the clicker. Feed him a treat when he reaches you. For a more enthusiastic come, run away at full speed as you call him. When he follows at a gallop, click, stop running, and give him a treat. The better your Pug gets at coming, the farther away he can be when you call him.

▓ Once your Pug understands the come cue, play with more people, each with a clicker and treats. Stand a short distance apart and take turns calling and running away. Click and treat in turn as he comes

Training sessions should be kept short and fun.

Socialize your Pug to kids early on, and supervise! Even though Pugs are hardy, children should not be rough with them.

to each of you. Gradually increase the distance until he comes flying to each person from a distance.

▓ When you and your Pug are ready to practice in wide-open spaces, attach a long line—a 20- to 50-foot leash—to your dog, so you can gather up your Pug if that

Did You Know? Once your Pug understands what behavior goes with a specific cue,
it is time to start weaning him off the food treats. At first, give a treat after each exercise. Then, start to give a treat only after every other exercise. Mix up the times when you offer a food reward and when you only offer praise. This way your dog will never know when he is going to receive food and praise or only praise.

taunting squirrel nearby is too much of a temptation. Then head to a practice area where there are less tempting distractions.

Heel: Heeling means that the dog walks beside his owner without pulling. It takes time and patience on your part to succeed at teaching the dog that you will not proceed unless he is walking calmly beside you. Pulling out ahead on the leash is definitely not acceptable.

▲ Begin by holding the leash in your left hand as your Pug sits beside your left leg. Move the loop end of the leash to your right hand, but keep your left hand short on the leash so that it keeps the dog close to you.

▲ Say "heel" and step forward on your left foot. Keep your Pug close to you and take three steps. Stop and have the dog sit next to you in what we now call the heel position. Praise verbally, but do not touch the dog.

Factor treats into your Pug's diet to prevent him from becoming overweight.

If you want to make your dog happy, create a digging spot where he's allowed to disrupt the earth. Encourage him to dig there by burying bones and toys, and helping him dig them up.

—Pat Miller, a certified pet dog trainer and owner of Peaceable Paws dog-training facility in Hagerstown, Md.

An obedience class will be useful if you are struggling to train your Pug dog.

Hesitate a moment and begin again with "heel," taking three steps and stopping, at which point the dog is told to sit again.

▲ Your goal here is to have your dog walk those three steps without pulling on the leash. Once he will walk calmly beside you for three steps without pulling, increase the number of steps you take to five. When he will walk politely beside you while you take five steps, you can increase the length of your walk to ten steps. Keep increasing the length of your stroll until your dog will walk quietly beside you without pulling for as long as you want him to heel. When you stop heeling, indicate to the dog that the exercise is over by petting him and

saying "OK, good dog." The "OK" is used as a release word, meaning that the exercise is finished, and the dog is free to relax.

▲ If you are dealing with a Pug who insists on pulling you around, simply put on your brakes and stand your ground until your Pug realizes that the two of you are not going anywhere until he is beside you and moving at your pace, not his. It may take some time just standing there to convince the dog that you are the leader, and you will be the one to decide on the direction and speed of your travel.

▲ Each time the dog looks up at you or slows down to give a slack leash between the two of you, quietly praise him and say,

JOIN OUR ONLINE

Pug Club

The best way to get your Pug well-socialized is to introduce him to different kinds of people and situations. Go online to download a socialization checklist at **DogChannel.com/Club-Pug**

"Good heel. Good dog." Eventually, your Pug will begin to respond, and within a few days he will be walking politely beside you without pulling on the leash. At first, the training sessions should be kept short and very positive; soon the dog will be able to walk nicely with you for increasingly longer distances. Remember to give the dog free time and the opportunity to run and play when you have finished heel practice.

TRAINING TIPS

If not properly socialized, managed, and trained, even well-bred Pugs will exhibit undesirable behaviors such as jumping up, barking, chasing, chewing, and other destructive behaviors. You can prevent these annoying habits and help your Pug become the perfect dog you're hoping for by following some basic training and behavior guidelines.

■ **Be consistent.** Consistency is important, not just in relation to what you allow your Pug to do (get on the sofa, perhaps) and not do (jump up on people), but also in the verbal and body language cues you use with your dog and in his daily routine.

■ **Be gentle but firm.** Positive training methods are very popular. Properly applied, dog-friendly methods are wonderfully effective, creating canine-human relationships based on respect and cooperation.

■ **Manage behavior.** All living things repeat behaviors that are rewarded. Behaviors that aren't reinforced will go away.

■ **Provide adequate exercise.** A tired dog is a well-behaved dog. Many behavior problems can be avoided, others resolved, by providing your Pug with enough exercise.

THE THREE-STEP PROGRAM

Perhaps it's too late to give your dog consistency, training, and management

from the start. Maybe he came from a Pug rescue or a shelter, or you didn't realize the importance of these tenets when he was a pup. He already may have learned some bad behaviors. Perhaps they're even part of his genetic package. Many problems can be modified with ease using the following three-step process for changing an unwanted behavior.

Step No. 1: Visualize the behavior you want from your dog. If you simply try to stop your Pug from doing something, you leave a behavior vacuum. You need to fill that vacuum with something, so your dog doesn't return to the same behavior or fill it with one that's even worse! If you're tired of your dog jumping up, decide what you'd prefer instead. A dog who greets people by sitting politely in front of them is a joy to own.

Step No. 2: Prevent your Pug from being rewarded for the behavior you don't want. Management to the rescue! When your Pug jumps up to greet you or get your attention, turn your back and step away to show him that jumping up no longer works to gain attention.

Step No. 3: Generously reinforce the desired behavior. Remember, dogs repeat behaviors that reward them. If your Pug no longer gets attention for jumping up and is heavily reinforced with attention and treats for sitting, he will offer sits instead of jumping, because sits get him what he wants.

COUNTER CONDITIONING

Behaviors that respond well to the three-step process are those where the dog does something in order to get good stuff. He jumps up to get attention. He countersurfs because he finds good stuff on counters. He nips at your hands to get you to play with him.

The three steps don't work well when you're dealing with behaviors that are based in strong emotion, such as aggression and fear, or with hardwired behaviors such as chasing prey. With these, you can change the emotional or hardwired response through counter conditioning—programming a new emotional or automatic response to the stimulus by giving it a new association. Here's how you would counter condition a Pug who chases after skateboarders when you're walking him on a leash.

Have a large supply of very high-value treats, such as canned chicken.

Station yourself with your Pug on a leash at a location where skateboarders will pass by at a subthreshold distance "X"—that is, where your Pug alerts but doesn't lunge and bark.

Wait for a skateboarder. The instant your Pug notices the skateboarder, feed him bits of chicken, nonstop, until the skateboarder is gone. Stop feeding him the chicken.

Repeat many times until, when the skateboarder appears, your Pug looks at you with a big grin as if to say, "Yay! Where's my chicken?" This is a conditioned emotional response, or CER.

When you have a consistent CER at X, decrease the distance slightly, perhaps minus 1 foot, and repeat until you consistently get the CER at this distance.

Continue decreasing the distance and obtaining a CER at each level, until a skateboarder zooming right past your Pug elicits the happy "Where's my chicken?" response. Now go back to distance X and add a second zooming skateboarder. Continue this process of gradual desensitization until your Pug doesn't turn a hair at a bevy of skateboarders.

Reward good behavior with a particularly high-value treat.

You'll know your hard work is worth the effort when you have a well-behaved adult Pug.

LEAVE IT ALONE

Pugs enjoy eating, which makes it easy to train them using treats. But there's a downside to that gastronomic gusto—some Pugs gobble down anything even remotely edible. This could include fresh food, rotten food, things that once were food, and any item that's ever been in contact with food. So, if you don't want your Pug gulping ground trash, teach it to leave things alone when told.

Place a tempting tidbit on the floor and cover it with your hand (gloved against teeth, if necessary). Say your cue word ("Leave it" or "Nah"). Your dog might lick, nibble and paw your hand—don't give in or you'll be rewarding bad manners.

Wait until dog moves away, then click or praise and give him a treat. Do not let the dog eat the temptation food that's on the floor, only the treats you give him. Repeat until dog stops moving toward the food temptation.

Lift your hand momentarily, letting the dog see the temptation. Say the cue word. Be ready to protect the treat but instantly reward your dog if he resists temptation. Repeat, moving your hand farther away and waiting longer before clicking and rewarding your Pug.

Increase the difficulty gradually—practice in different locations, add new temptations, drop treats from standing height, drop several at a time and step away.

Remember to use your cue word, so your Pug dog will know what it's expected to do. Always reward good behavior! Rehearse this skill daily for a week. After that, you'll have enough real-life opportunities to practice.

BAD HABITS

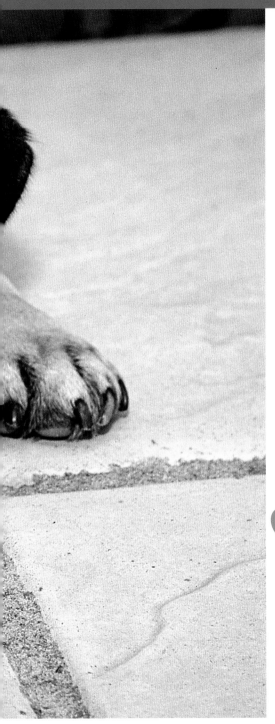

Discipline—training one to act in accordance with rules—brings order to life. It is as simple as that. Without discipline, particularly in a group society, chaos reigns supreme, and the group will eventually perish. Humans and canines are social animals and need some form of discipline in order to function effectively. Dogs need discipline in their lives in order to understand how their pack (you and other family members) functions and how they must act in order to survive.

Luckily, puppies are little sponges, waiting to soak up whatever information they can, be it bad habits or good manners. Start training early, and you can control your Pug's behaviors.

The following behavioral problems are the ones that owners most commonly encounter. Every dog is unique and every situation is unique. Because behavioral abnormalities are the leading reason for owners' abandoning their pets, we hope that you will make a valiant effort to solve your Pug's problems.

Did You Know?

Anxiety can make a dog really miserable. Living in a world with scary, vaporous monsters and suspected Pug-eaters roaming the streets has to be pretty nerve-wracking. The good news is that timid dogs are not doomed to be forever ruled by fear. Owners who understand a timid Pug's needs can help him build self-confidence and a more optimistic view of life.

NIP NIPPING

As puppies start to teethe, they feel the need to sink their teeth into anything—unfortunately, that includes your fingers, arms, hair, toes, whatever happens to be available. You may find this behavior cute for about the first five seconds—until you feel just how sharp those puppy teeth are. This is something you want to discourage immediately and consistently with a firm "No!" (or whatever number it takes for your dog to understand that you mean business) and replace your finger with an appropriate chew toy.

STOP THAT WHINING

A puppy will often cry, whine, whimper, howl, or make some type of commotion when he is left alone. This is basically his way of calling out for attention, of calling out to make sure that you know he is there, and that you have not forgotten about him. He feels insecure when he is left alone; for example, when you are out of the house and he is in his crate, or when you are in another part of the house and he cannot see you. The noise he is making is an expression of the anxiety he feels at being alone, so he needs to be taught that being alone is OK. You are not actually training your dog to stop making noise, you are training him to feel comfortable when he is alone and thus removing the need to make the noise.

This is where the crate with a cozy blanket and a toy comes in handy. You want to know that your pup is safe when you are not there

Pug puppies are adorable. Their bad habits aren't, though.

to supervise, and you know that he will be safe in his crate rather than roaming freely about the house. In order for the pup to stay in his crate without making a fuss, he needs to be comfortable in his crate. It is extremely important that the crate is never used as a form of punishment, or the pup will have a negative association with the crate.

Accustom the pup to the crate in short, gradually increasing intervals of time, maybe with a treat, and stay in the room with him. If he cries or makes a fuss, do not go to him, but stay in his sight. Gradually he will realize that staying in his crate is all right with-

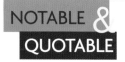

NOTABLE & QUOTABLE

Pugs like to learn by doing. Pugs do things at their own speed. I've found that, on average, when teaching a new command, Pugs are good for about fifteen minutes before they need a break.

—Lyle Reed, owner of Mind of Their Own Dog Training, in Roseville, Calif.

out your help, and it will not be so traumatic for him when you are not around. You may want to leave the radio on softly when you leave the house; the sound of human voices can be comforting to him.

CHEW ON THIS

The national canine pastime is chewing! Every dog loves to sink his "canines" into a tasty bone, but most anything will do! Dogs need to chew to massage their gums, to make their new teeth feel better, and to exercise their jaws. This is a natural behavior deeply imbedded in all things canine. Our role as smart owners is not to stop chewing, but to redirect it to positive, chew-worthy objects. Be an informed owner and purchase proper chew toys for your Pug, like strong nylon bones. Be sure that these chew toys are safe and durable because your dog's safety is at risk.

The best answer to a chewing problems is prevention: That is, put your shoes, handbags, and other tasty objects in their proper places

SMART TIP!

The golden rule of dog training is simple. For each "question" (cue), there is only one correct answer (reaction). One cue equals one reaction. Keep practicing the cue until the dog reacts correctly without hesitation. Be repetitive but not monotonous. Dogs get bored just as people do; a bored dog's attention will not be focused on the lesson.

(out of the reach of the growing canine mouth). Direct your puppy to his toys whenever you see him tasting the furniture legs or the leg of your pants. Make a noise to attract your pup's attention, and immediately escort him to his chew toy and engage him with the toy for at least four minutes, praising and encouraging him all the while.

NO MORE JUMPING

Jumping up is a dog's friendly way of saying hello, and some energetic Pugs may get in this habit. Some dog owners do not mind when their dog jumps up, which is

Dogs were born to chew. Redirect your Pug's chewing to more appropriate items, such as toys.

fine for them, but Pugs owners should discourage this for many reasons. The problem arises when guests come to the house, and the dog greets them in the same manner—whether they like it or not! However friendly the greeting may be, chances are your visitors will not appreciate being jumped on by your Pug. Your dog will not be able to distinguish upon whom he can jump and whom he cannot.

Pick a command such as "Off!" (avoid using "down" because you will use that for the dog to lie down) and tell him "Off!" when he jumps up. Place him on the ground on all fours and have him sit, praising him the whole time. Always lavish him with praise and petting when he is in the "sit" position. That way, you are still giving him a warm, affectionate greeting, because you are as excited to see him as he is to see you!

UNWANTED BARKING MUST GO

Barking is a dog's way of talking. It can be somewhat frustrating because it is not easy to tell what a dog means by his bark: is he excited, happy, frightened, angry? Whatever it is that the dog is trying to say, he should not be punished for barking. It is only when the barking becomes excessive, and when the excessive barking becomes a bad habit, that the behavior needs to be modified.

If an intruder came into your home in the middle of the night and the dog barked a warning, wouldn't you be pleased? You would probably deem your dog a hero, a wonderful guardian and protector of the home. On the other hand, if a friend drops by unexpectedly and rings the doorbell

> **Did You Know?**
>
> **Dogs do not understand our language.** They can be trained, however, to react to a certain sound, at a certain volume. Never use your dog's name during a reprimand, as he might come to associate it with a bad thing!

Your Pug may howl, whine, or otherwise vocalize his displeasure at your leaving the house and his being left alone. This is a normal case of separation anxiety, but there are things that can be done to eliminate this problem. Your dog needs to learn that he will be fine on his own for a while and that he will not wither away if he isn't attended to every minute of the day.

In fact, constant attention can lead to separation anxiety in the first place. If you are endlessly coddling and cuddling your Pug, he will come to expect this from you all of the time, and it will be more traumatic for him when you are not there.

To help minimize separation anxiety, make your entrances and exits as low-key as possible. Do not give your Pug a long, drawn-out goodbye, and do not lavish him with hugs and kisses when you return. This will only make him miss you more when you are away. Another thing you can try is to give your dog a treat when you leave; this will keep him occupied, it will keep his mind off the fact that you just left, and it will help him associate your leaving with a pleasant experience.

You may have to accustom your Pug to being left alone in intervals, much like when you introduced him to his crate. Of course, when your

dog starts whimpering as you approach the door, your first instinct will be to run to him and comfort him, but don't do it! Eventually, he will adjust and be just fine if you take it in small steps. His anxiety stems from being placed in an unfamiliar situation; by familiarizing him with being alone he will learn that he is OK.

When your Pug is alone in the house, confine him in his crate or a designated dog-proof area of the house. This should be the area in which he sleeps, so he will already feel comfortable there and this should make him feel more at ease when he is alone. This is just one of the many examples in which a crate is an invaluable tool for you and your Pug, and another reinforcement of why your dog should view his crate as a happy place, a place of his own.

and is greeted with a sudden sharp bark, you would probably be annoyed at the dog. But isn't it just the same behavior? The dog does not know any better—unless he sees who is at the door and it is someone he knows, he will bark to announce that his (and your) territory is being threatened. While your friend is not posing a threat, it is all the same to the dog. Barking is his means of letting you know that there is an intrusion, whether friend or foe, on your property. This type of barking is instinctive and should not be discouraged.

Excessive habitual barking, however, is a problem that should be corrected early on. As your Pug grows up, you will be able to tell when his barking is purposeful and when it is for no reason. Soon, you will be able to distinguish your dog's different barks and with what they are associated. For example, the bark when someone comes to the door will be different from the bark when he is excited to see you. It is similar to a person's tone of voice, except that the dog has to rely totally on tone of voice because he does not have the benefit of using words. An incessant barker will be evident at an early age.

There are some things that encourage a dog to bark. For example, if your dog barks nonstop for a few minutes and you give him a treat to quiet him, he believes that you are rewarding him for barking. He will

SMART TIP!

Do not carry your dog to his potty area. Lead him there on a leash or, better yet, encourage him to follow you to the spot. If you start carrying him, you might end up doing this routine forever and your dog will have the satisfaction of having trained you.

If your Pug is a barker, reward him when he keeps quiet, and he'll learn to stop making so much noise.

Stage false departures. Pick up your car keys and put on your coat, then put them away and go about your routine. Do this several times a day, ignoring your dog while you do it. Soon his reaction to these triggers will decrease.

—September Morn, a dog trainer and behavior specialist in Bellingham, Wash.

associate barking with getting a treat, and will keep doing it until he is rewarded.

STOP FOOD STEALING AND BEGGING

Is your dog devising ways of stealing food from your cupboards? If so, you must answer the following questions: Is your Pug hungry, or is he constantly famished, like every other chowhound? Face it, some dogs are more food-motivated than others; some dogs are totally obsessed by a slab of brisket and can only think of their next meal. Food stealing is terrific fun and always yields a great reward—food, glorious food!

The owner's goal, therefore, is to make the "reward" less rewarding, even startling! Plant a shaker can (an empty can with coins inside) on the table so that it catches your pooch off-guard. There are other devices that will surprise a dog when he is looking for a midafternoon snack. Remote-control devices, though not the first choice of some trainers, allow the correction to come from the object instead of the owner. These devices are also useful to keep the snacking dog from napping on furniture that is forbidden.

Just like food stealing, begging is a favorite pastime of hungry puppies with that same reward—food! No dog looks as desperate and appealing as a Pug on his twos! Dogs quickly learn that humans love that pose and that their selfish owners keep the "good food" for themselves. Why would humans dine on kibble when they can cook up sausages and kielbasa? Begging is a conditioned response related to a specific stimulus, time, and place. The sounds of the kitchen, cans, and bottles opening, crinkling bags, and the smell of food in preparation will excite the chowhound and soon the paws are in the air!

Did You Know?

Some natural remedies for separation anxiety are reputed to have calming effects, but check with your vet before use. Flower essence remedies are water-based extracts of different plants, which are stabilized and preserved with brandy. A human dose is only a few drops, so seek advice from a natural healing practitioner on proper dosage for your Pug.

The solution to stopping this behavior is to never give in to a beggar, no matter how cute or desperate! You only reward the dog for jumping up, whining, and rubbing his nose into you by giving him food. Ignore him, and you eventually will force the behavior into extinction. The behavior likely will get worse before it disappears, so be sure there aren't any softies in the family who give in to your dog every time he whimpers, "More, please."

POOP ALERT!

Feces eating, aka coprophagia, is the most disgusting behavior that a dog can engage in, yet to the dog it is perfectly normal. Vets have found that diets with low digestibility, containing relatively low levels of fiber, and high levels of starch, increase coprophagia. Therefore, high-fiber diets may decrease the likelihood of dogs' eating feces. To discourage this behavior, feed food that is nutritionally complete and in the proper amount. If changes in your Pug's diet do not seem to work, and no medical cause can be found, you will have to modify the behavior through environmental control before it becomes a habit.

It's difficult to say no to your cute little Pug, but begging must be discouraged.

There are some tricks you can try, such as adding an unpleasant-tasting substance to the feces to make them unpalatable or adding something to the dog's food which will make it unpleasant tasting after it passes through the dog. The best way to prevent your dog from eating his stool is to make it unavailable—clean up after he eliminates and remove any stool from the yard. If it is not there, he cannot eat it.

Never reprimand a dog for stool eating, as this rarely impresses the dog. Vets recommend distracting the dog while he is in the act of stool eating. Another option is to muzzle the dog when he is in the yard to relieve himself; this usually is effective within thirty to sixty days. Coprophagia most frequently is seen in pups six to twelve months of age, and usually disappears around the dog's first birthday.

GARBAGE GOBBLIN'

Pugs enjoy eating, which makes it easy to train them using treats. But there's a downside to that gastronomic gusto—some Pugs gobble down anything even remotely edible. This could include fresh food, rotten food, things that once were food, and any item that's ever been in contact with food. So, if you don't want your Pug gulping ground-trash, teach him to leave things alone when told.

Place a tempting tidbit on the floor and cover it with your hand (gloved against teeth, if necessary). Say your cue word ("Leave it" or "Nah"). Your dog might lick, nibble, and paw your hand—don't give in or you'll be rewarding bad manners.

Pugs are smart, and quickly will learn to avoid bad behavior.

Wait until your dog moves away, then click or praise, and give him a treat. Do not let the dog eat the temptation food that's on the floor, only the treats you give it. Repeat until your dog stops moving toward the food temptation.

Lift your hand momentarily, letting your dog see the temptation. Say the cue word. Be ready to protect the treat but instantly reward your dog if he resists temptation. Repeat, moving your hand farther away and waiting longer before clicking and rewarding your Pug.

Increase the difficulty gradually—practice in different locations, add new temptations, drop treats from standing height, drop several at a time and step away.

Remember to use your cue word, so your dog will know what he's expected to do. Always reward good behavior! Rehearse this skill daily for a week. After that, you'll have enough real-life opportunities to practice.

NOTABLE & QUOTABLE

The purpose of puppy classes is for puppies to learn how to learn. The pups get the training along the way, but the training is almost secondary.

—*professional trainer Peggy Shunick Duezabou of Helena, Mont.*

PLAY

Think your Pug is a lap dog? Think again! When it comes to dog sports, the stout and hardy Pug is just as ready, willing and able to participate as a larger or more athletic breed. Given early socialization, conditioning, and training, your Pug can tear up the dog sports field, be your best walking or hiking companion, rack up points in the show ring, or spread love as a therapy dog.

EXERCISE

All dogs need exercise to keep them physically and mentally healthy. An inactive dog is a fat dog, with the accompanying likelihood of joint strain or torn ligaments. Inactive dogs also are prone to mischief—and may do anything to relieve their boredom. This often leads to behavior problems, such as chewing or barking. Regular daily exercise like daily walks and short play sessions will help keep your Pug slim, trim, and happy.

Provide your Pug with interactive play that stimulates both mind and body. It's a good idea to have a daily period of one-on-one play, especially with a puppy or young dog. Continue this type of interaction throughout your dog's life, and you will build a lasting bond. Even oldsters that are slowing down a bit need the stimulation that activity provides.

Did You Know? The Fédération Internationale Cynologique is the world kennel club that governs dog shows in Europe and elsewhere around the world.

Before You Begin
Because of the physical demands of sporting activities, a Pug puppy shouldn't begin officially training until he is done growing. That doesn't mean, though, that you can't begin socializing him to sports. Talk to your vet about what age is appropriate.

If your Pug is older or overweight, consult your veterinarian about how much and what type of exercise he needs. Usually, a ten- to fifteen-minute walk once a day is a good start. As the pounds start to drop off, your dog's energy level will rise, and you can increase the amount of daily exercise.

Whether a dog is trained in the structured environment of a class or alone with his owner at home, there also are many sporting activities that can bring fun and rewards to owner and dog once they have mastered basic control.

OBEDIENCE TRIALS

Obedience trials in the United States trace back to the early 1930s, when organized obedience training was developed to demonstrate how well dog and owner could work together. The pioneer of obedience trials is Helen Whitehouse Walker, a Standard Poodle fancier, who designed a series of exercises after the Associated Sheep, Police Army Dog Society of Great Britain. Since the days of Walker, obedience trials have grown by leaps and bounds, and today more than 2,000 trials are held in the United States every year, with more than 100,000 dogs competing. Any registered American Kennel Club or Indefinite Listing Privilege dog can enter an obedience trial, regardless of con-

Pugs love to play outdoors. Keep in mind that they overheat easily, even in cold weather, so take plenty of breaks so you both can cool down.

formational disqualifications or neutering.

Obedience trials are divided into three levels of progressive difficulty. At the first level, the Novice, dogs compete for the title of Companion Dog; at the intermediate level, the Open, dogs compete for a Companion Dog Excellent title; and at the Advanced level, dogs compete for a Utility Dog title. Classes are sub-divided into "A" (for beginners) and "B" (for more experienced handlers). A perfect score at any level is 200, and a dog must score 170 or better to earn a "leg," of which three are needed to earn the title. To earn points, the dog must score more

NOTABLE & QUOTABLE

Start walking these guys as puppies, and keep them in good shape as they mature. It's much easier to keep a dog in good shape than to get a dog in good shape.

—Robin Downing, D.V.M., from Windsor, Colo.

than fifty percent of the available points in each exercise; the possible points range from twenty to forty.

Once a dog has earned the UD title, he can compete with other proven obedience dogs for the coveted title of Utility Dog Excellent, which requires that the dog win "legs" in ten shows. In 1977, the title Obedience Trial Champion was established by the AKC. Utility Dogs who earn legs in Open B and Utility B earn points toward their Obedience Trial Champion title. To become an OTCh., a dog needs to earn 100 points, which requires three first places in Open B and Utility under three different judges.

The Grand Prix of obedience trials, the AKC National Obedience Invitational, gives qualifying Utility Dogs the chance to win the newest and highest title: National Obedience Champion. Only the top twenty-five ranked obedience dogs, plus any dog ranked in the top three in his breed, are allowed to compete.

AGILITY TRIALS

Agility is one of the most popular dog sports out there. Training your Pug in agility will boost his confidence and teach him to focus on you.

In agility competition, the dog and handler move through a prescribed course, negotiating a series of obstacles that may include jumps (a Pug's least favorite), tunnels (his favorite), a dog walk, an A-frame, a seesaw, a pause table, and weave poles. Dogs who run through a course without refusing any obstacles, going off course or knocking down any bars, all within a set time, get a qualifying score. Dogs with a certain number of qualifying scores in their given division (Novice, Open, Excellent, and Mach, at AKC trials) earn an agility title.

Several different organizations recognize agility events. AKC-sanctioned agility events are the most common. The United States Dog Agility Association also sanctions agility trials, as does the United

Don't believe the myth that Pugs are couch potatoes. OK, it's mostly true, but Pugs also can do well in sports, like agility.

Activities don't have to be strenuous. Take your pug with you on your favorite outdoor adventure.

Kennel Club. The rules are different for each of these organizations, but the principles are the same.

When Pugs compete in agility, they usually jump at a height of only 4 or 8 inches, depending on the height of the dog. With the exception of the jumps, Pugs are expected to negotiate the other obstacles on

the course at the same height and distance as other breeds (the one exception is the pause table, which is lowered). Because each division of agility is subdivided by jump height, Pugs compete for ribbons against other dogs their own size.

When your Pug starts his agility training, he will begin by learning to negotiate each individual obstacle while on-leash, as you guide him. Eventually, you will steer him through a few obstacles in a row, one after another. Once he catches on that this is how agility works, he can run a short course off-leash. One day, you'll see the light go on in your Pug's eyes as he figures out that he should look to you for guidance as he runs through the agility course. Your job will be to tell him which obstacles to take next, using your voice and your body as signals.

SMART TIP!

Most Pugs get along well with other pets, especially if introduced while young. Use caution when your Pug meets a new cat, though, as the Pug's prominent eyes are vulnerable to sudden claw-swipes. Hold your Pug so he doesn't playfully leap onto the cat, frightening the feline into self-protection.

RALLY BEHIND RALLY

Rally is a sport that combines competition obedience with elements of agility, but is less demanding than either one of these activities. Rally was designed keeping the average dog owner in mind, and is easier than many other sporting activities.

At a rally event, dogs and handlers are asked to move through ten to twenty different stations, depending on the level of competition. The stations are marked by numbered signs, which tell the handler the exercise to be performed at this station. The exercises vary from making different types of turns to changing pace.

Dogs can earn rally titles as they get better at the sport and move through the different levels. The titles to strive for are Rally Novice, Rally Advanced, Rally Excellent, and Rally Advanced Excellent.

To get your Pug puppy prepared to do rally competition, focus on teaching him basic obedience, for starters. Your dog must know the five basic obedience cues—sit, down, stay, come, and heel—and perform them well before he's ready for rally. Next, you can enroll your dog in a rally class. Although he must be at least six months of age to compete in rally, you can start training long before his six-month birthday.

Dog shows may not be for your Pug, but plenty of other events are tailored just for him!

SHOW DOGS

When you purchase your Pug puppy, you must make it clear to the breeder whether you want one just as a lovable companion and pet, or if you hope to be buying a Pug with show prospects. No reputable breeder will sell you a puppy and tell you that the dog will definitely be

NOTABLE & QUOTABLE

Pugs love to please. They are known as clown dogs. When you look at them, it brings a smile to your face, and they know it!

—Tina Seri, president of the Pugs 'N Pals rescue group
in Orange County, Calif.

show quality because so much can go wrong during the early months of a puppy's development. If you do plan to show, what you hopefully will have acquired is a puppy with show "potential."

To the novice, exhibiting a Pug in the ring may look easy, but it takes a lot of hard work and devotion to win at a show such as the Westminster Kennel Club dog show, not to mention a little luck, too!

The first concept that the canine novice learns when watching a dog show is that each dog first competes against members of his own breed. Once the judge has selected the best member of each breed (Best of Breed) the chosen dog will compete with other dogs in its group. Finally, the dogs chosen first in each group will compete for Best in Show.

The second concept that you must understand is that the dogs are not actually compared against one another. The judge compares each dog against the breed standard, the written description of the ideal specimen that is approved by the AKC. While some early breed standards were indeed based on specific dogs that were famous or popular, many dedicated enthusiasts say that a perfect specimen as described in the standard has never walked

into a show ring, has never been bred and, to the woe of dog breeders around the globe, does not exist. Breeders attempt to get as close to this ideal as possible with every litter, but theoretically the "perfect" dog is so elusive that it is impossible. (And if the perfect dog were born, breeders and judges probably would never agree that he was indeed perfect.)

If you are interested in exploring the world of conformation, your best bet is to join your local breed club or the national (or parent) club, the Pug Dog Club of America. These clubs often host regional and national specialties, shows only for Pugs, which can include conformation as well as obedience

In 1996, Mushu needed a home. His owner was moving and had signed a lease at a complex that wouldn't accept dogs. So, he placed an ad in the local paper.

At the same time, Cristie Miele, an animal trainer for Animal Actors of Hollywood, was looking for a Pug for an upcoming movie, *Men In Black.* "There were no trained Pugs in the business," she recalls, and so she was actively searching for a suitable dog to begin training. "I needed an outgoing, happy-go-lucky dog."

When she called Mushu's owner, he suggested she come out and take a look at the one-year-old fawn Pug. Mushu was just what Miele was looking for.

Before Mushu could begin filming for the movie (as an alien posing as a Pug named Frank), "He had to learn the movie dog basics: stay, bark on cue, hit a mark, sit, and lie down." Six years later when the sequel, *MIB II,* was to be filmed, Mushu had to learn a few more things: "He had to carry things in his mouth, climb on top of an alien, wear a headset, and shake water off on cue."

Miele concedes that all the movie fame and glory might have gone to Mushu's head. After a world tour that included appearances in Berlin, and Paris, Mushu didn't want to stop. "If he had his choice, he would go somewhere everyday," Miele says. And who wouldn't want to if you got to fly first class and travel in stretch limos? "He's getting a little spoiled," Miele admits.

Sports are physically demanding. Have your vet do a full examination of your Pug to rule out joint problems, heart disease, eye aliments, and other maladies. Once you get the all-clear healthwise, start having fun in your new sporting life!

and field trials. Even if you have no intention of competing with your Pug, a specialty is a like a festival for lovers of the breed who congregate to share their favorite topic: Pugs! Clubs also send out newsletters, and some organize training days and seminars in order that people may learn more about their chosen breed. To locate the breed club closest to you, contact the AKC, which furnishes the rules and regulations for all of these events, plus general dog registration and other basic requirements of dog ownership.

DANCING DOGS

The competitive dog sport of musical freestyle has three classes at three different levels. The classes are Individual (one handler, one dog), Brace (two handlers, two dogs), and Team (three or more handlers, each with a dog). Pugs may compete in on- or off-leash divisions, but all dogs must qualify from the off-leash division to move on to the masters division. Titles a dog can earn are Musical Freestyle Dog, Musical Freestyle Excellent, and Musical Freestyle Master.

THERAPEUTIC PUGS

Therapy work offers a special kind of satisfaction, the gratification of bringing pleasure simply through your dog's presence. If you like helping people, you and your Pug can bring happiness and laughter to people who are confined to hospitals and nursing homes. Therapy-dog visits are a wonderful way for you to share the enjoyment of Pug ownership with others. Petting your dog can ease the loneliness of a widower in a nursing home, lower the blood pressure of a hospital patient, and win big grins and belly laughs from children in a cancer ward.

Your therapy Pug must be clean and flea-free, and exhibit good manners. No food stealing or potty accidents! He must pass a temperament test to ensure that he's suited to this type of work. A sweet, tolerant, fearless disposition is ideal because therapy work involves encounters with new or unusual places, people, and equipment. Both of you will attend training classes before visits begin. Be sure to take normal precautions against falls from aged, shaky hands or run-ins with wheelchairs or walkers. A short leash attached to a harness will help you keep control.

CANINE GOOD CITIZEN

If obedience work sounds too regimented but you'd still like your Pug to have a title, prepare him for the Canine Good Citizen test. This program is sponsored by the AKC, with

Get outdoors and have fun in doggie sports.

tests administered by local dog clubs, private trainers, and 4-H clubs.

To earn a CGC title, your Pug must be well-groomed and demonstrate the manners that all good dogs should exhibit. The CGC test requires a dog to perform the sit, down, stay, and come commands, react appropriately to other dogs and distractions, allow a stranger to approach it, sit politely for petting, walk nicely on a loose lead, move through a crowd without going wild, calm down after play or praise, and sit still for examination by the judge. Rules are posted on www.akc.org

Otis was a working Pug. The little fawn male with a double curl in his tail is thought to have been the first Pug ever to be trained as a hearing service dog. Though Otis passed away in June 2002 after more than ten years of service, the little dog set a standard for other Pugs to follow.

Otis was special from the beginning. During a routine scouting of a local animal shelter for hearing dog prospects, Sheila O'Brien, marketing director for the National Education for Assistance Dog Services Inc. in Princeton, Mass., spotted a three-year-old fawn Pug. O'Brien tested the little dog at the shelter to see if he had the traits necessary to be a hearing dog prospect. He did. "I brought him home that evening," she relates.

"We'd worked with Pug mixes before, but Otis was the first purebred Pug to come through our program," remembers Brian Jennings, trainer at NEADS. Jennings notes that it is always difficult to find small dogs for the program. "If they have really sweet temperaments, they're often scooped up by pet owners" before NEADS has an opportunity to see or evaluate them, Jennings says. When Otis came to NEADS, he was good with people and children, self-confident, and a one-person dog—all good hearing dog qualities. "He wasn't [initially] as good with sounds—at the beginning he'd rather sit in someone's lap," chuckles Jennings. "But we made a game of it," he recounts, and Otis quickly caught on. Being a Pug, Otis was very food motivated, too, which made training go rapidly.

"He was a wonderful little dog," says Jennings, who decided Otis would be a perfect match for Herbert Weiss of Monroe Township, N.J. "We try to match the dog's personality with the person's," he explains. "Herbert is an easygoing guy, a real people person. He could easily be talking to people in public and forget he had a dog." For the gregarious Pug who loved to be in social settings, the pairing was perfect.

In May 1991 at NEADS' service dog graduation, seven assistance dogs and two hearing dogs graduated. All were Golden and Labrador Retrievers—except for one proud Pug, Otis.

"Otis was a remarkable animal," affirms Herbert's wife, Barbara. "At times he frightened us because he was so intelligent. He loved children. And his work was unbelievable."

As a trained hearing dog, Otis alerted Herbert to various sounds by lightly pawing at Herbert's leg, running to the sound, running back to Herbert, running back to the sound, until Herbert acknowledged that he'd heard the sound. Otis was trained to alert Herbert to many sounds, including a knock at the door, the doorbell, the phone ringing, a name call (if Barbara or someone else was calling Herbert's name, Otis would run and get him) and a one-way alert for the smoke alarm. (In potentially dangerous situations [i.e., a fire], the hearing dog gives an alert but does not run to the source of the sound. This one-

way alert lets the owner know that the sound is dangerous and that he or she should leave the building or home at once.)

Otis also alerted Herbert to the alarm clock in the morning. "When the alarm rang, Otis would give Herb a face wash," laughs Barbara. "And Otis didn't listen to, 'OK. Later!' There wasn't a snooze button on him!"

Otis was trained to listen for oncoming cars, too, and would stop Herbert from crossing a street if he heard a car coming from behind. Otis also learned on his own to alert Herbert to the microwave oven's buzzer.

As a service dog, Otis went everywhere with Herbert—to services, on the airplane, in grocery stores, and to volunteer activities. Wearing his orange vest, which indicated he was a certified hearing dog, Otis worked continuously—nearly up until the day he passed away. Even though Herbert had retired Otis after the Pug lost his hearing and eventually his eyesight, Barbara relates that Otis continued to work. "He was Herb's pal. He followed Herb to the very end." She adds, "He was a remarkable animal. I don't think anyone can wear his shoes."

To find more information about this popular dog breed, contact the following organizations. They will be glad to help you dig deeper into the world of Pugs.

American Kennel Club: The AKC website offers information and links to conformation, tracking, rally, obedience and agility programs, and member clubs. www.akc.org

Ben Friedman's Pug Parties: This site lists Pug events at Joe's Sports Bar in Chicago. www.pugparty.com

Canadian Kennel Club: Our northern neighbor's oldest kennel club is similar to the AKC in the states. www.ckc.ca

Love on a Leash: There are more than 900 members of this pet therapy organization. www.loveonaleash.org

North American Dog Agility Council: This site provides links to clubs, trainers, and agility trainers in the United States and Canada. www.nadac.com

Pug Dog Club of America: The PDCA site includes breed history information, breeder referrals and much more. www.pugs.org

Pug Parliament: This annual Pug event in Overland Park, Kan., is always fun for Pugs and their owners. www.pugspeak.com

Pug.meetup.com: This site has meet-up information for cities all across the United States. Pug.meetup.com

PugRescue.com: This website has several links to rescues across the country. www.pugrescue.com

Therapy Dogs Inc.: Get your Pug involved in therapy. www.therapydogs.com

Therapy Dogs International: Find more therapy dog info here: www.tdi-dog.org

United Kennel Club: The UKC offers several of the events offered by the AKC, including agility, conformation, and obedience. In addition, the UKC offers competitions in hunting and dog sport (companion and protective events). Both the UKC and the AKC offer programs for juniors, ages two to eighteen. www.ukcdogs.com

United States Dog Agility Association: The USDAA has information on training, clubs, and events in the United States, Canada, Mexico, and overseas. www.usdaa.com

World Canine Freestyle Organization: Dancing with your dog is fun! www.worldcaninefreestyle.org

it's a **Fact**

The **American Kennel Club** was started in 1884. It is America's oldest kennel club. The **United Kennel Club** is the second oldest in the United States. It began registering dogs in 1898.

BOARDING

So you want to take a family vacation—and you want to include all members of the family. You usually make arrangements for accommodations ahead of time anyway, but this is imperative when traveling with a dog. You do not want to make an overnight stop at the only place around for miles and find out that the hotel doesn't allow dogs. Also, you do not want to reserve a room for your family without confirming that you are traveling with a dog because, if it is against the hotel's policy, you may not have a place to stay.

Alternatively, if you are traveling and choose not to bring your Pug, you will have to make arrangements for him. Some options are to bring him to a family member or a neighbor, have a trusted friend stop by often or stay at your house, or bring your dog to a reputable boarding kennel.

If you choose to board him at a kennel, visit in advance to see the facilities and check how clean they are, and where the dogs are kept. Talk to some of the employees and see how they treat the dogs—do they spend time with the dogs, play with them, exercise them, etc.? Also find out the kennel's policy on vaccinations and what they require. This is for all of the dogs' safety because when dogs are kept together, there is a greater risk of diseases being passed from dog to dog.

Pug people can be a fun social bunch to hang out with and talk about all things Pug!

HOME STAFFING

For the Pug parent who works all day, a pet sitter or dog walker may be the perfect solution for the lonely Pug longing for a mid-day stroll. Dog owners can approach local high schools or community centers if they don't know of a neighbor who is interested in a part-time commitment. Interview potential dog walkers and consider their experience with dogs, as well as your Pug's rapport with the candidate. (Pugs are excellent judges of character, unless there's liver involved.) Always check references before entrusting your dog and home to a new dog walker.

For an owner's long-term absence, such as a business trip or vacation, many Pug owners welcome the services of a pet sitter. It's usually less stressful on the dog to stay home with a pet sitter than to be boarded in a kennel. Pet sitters also may be more affordable than a week's stay at a full-service doggie day care.

Pet sitters must be even more reliable than dog walkers because the dog is depending on his surrogate owner for all of his needs for an extended period. Owners are advised to hire a certified pet sitter through the National Association of Professional Pet Sitters, which can be accessed online at www.petsitters.org. NAPPS provides online and toll-free pet sitter locator services. The nonprofit organization only certifies serious-minded, professional individuals who are knowledgeable in canine behavior, nutrition, health, and safety. Always keep your Pug's best interest at heart when planning a trip.

SCHOOL'S IN SESSION

Puppy kindergarten, which is usually open to dogs between three to six months of age, allows puppies to learn and socialize with other dogs and people in a structured setting. Classes help your Pug enjoy going places with you, and help your dog become a well-behaved member at public gatherings that include other dogs. They prepare him for adult obedience classes, as well as for life.

The problem with most puppy kindergarten classes is that they only occur one night a week. What about during the rest of the week?

If you're at home all week, you may be able to find other places to take your puppy, but you have to be careful about dog parks and other places where just any dog can go. An experience with a bully can undo all the good your classes have done, or worse, end in tragedy.

If you work, your puppy may be home alone all day, a tough situation for a Pug. Chances are he can't hold himself that long, so your potty training will be undermined unless you're just aiming to teach him to use an indoor potty. And chances are, by the time you come home, he'll be bursting with energy, and you may start thinking that he's hyperactive.

The answer for the professional with a Pug is doggie day care. Most larger cities have some sort of day care, whether it's a boarding kennel that keeps your dog in a run or a full-service day care that offers training, play time, and even spa facilities. They range from a person who keeps a few dogs at his home to a state-of-the-art facility built just for dogs. Many of the more sophisticated doggie day cares offer webcams so you can see your dog throughout the day. Things to look for:

- escape-proof facilities, including a buffer between the dogs and any doors
- inoculation requirements for new dogs
- midday meals for young dogs
- obedience training (if offered), using reward-based methods
- safe and comfortable time-out areas for sleeping
- screening of dogs for aggression
- small groups of similar sizes and ages
- toys and playground equipment, such as tunnels
- trained staff, with an adequate number to supervise the dogs (no more than ten to fifteen dogs per person)
- a webcam

SMART TIP!

Remember to keep your dog's leash slack when interacting with other dogs. It is not unusual for a dog to pick out one or two canine neighbors to dislike. If you know there's bad blood, step off to the side and put a barrier, such as a parked car, between the dogs. If there are no barriers to be had, move to the side of the walkway, cue your dog to sit, stay, and watch you until his nemesis passes; then continue your walk.

CAR TRAVEL

You should accustom your Pug to riding in a car at an early age. You may or may not take him in the car often, but at the very least he will need to go to the vet, and you do not want these trips to be traumatic for the dog or troublesome for you. The safest way for a dog to ride in the car is in his crate. If he uses a crate in the house, you can use the same crate for travel.

Another option is a specially made safety harness for dogs, which straps the Pug in the car much like a seat belt would. Do not let the dog roam loose in the vehicle—this is very dangerous! If you should stop short, your dog can be thrown and injured. If the dog starts climbing on you and pestering you while you are driving, you will not be able to concentrate on the road. It is an unsafe situation for everyone—human and canine.

For long trips, stop often to let your dog relieve himself. Take along whatever you need to clean up after him, including some paper towels and perhaps some old bath towels for use should he have an accident in the car or suffer from motion sickness.

Did You Know?

The dog run is one of the few urban spaces where a dog can be off-leash. To enter most dog parks, dogs must be fully vaccinated and healthy, and females must not be in season.

IDENTIFICATION

Your Pug is your valued companion and friend. That is why you always keep a close eye on him, and you have made sure that he cannot escape from the yard or wriggle out of his collar and run away from you. However, accidents can happen and there may come a time when your dog unexpectedly gets separated from you. If this should occur, the first thing on your mind will be finding him. Proper identification, including an ID tag, a tattoo, and possibly a microchip, will increase the chances of his being returned to you safely and quickly.

An ID tag on a collar or harness is the primary means of pet identification (and ID licenses are required in many communities, anyway). Although inexpensive and easy to read, collars and ID tags can come off or be taken off.

A microchip doesn't get lost. Containing a unique ID number which can be read by scanners, the microchip is embedded underneath a dog's skin. It's invaluable for identifying lost or stolen pets. However, to be effective, the microchip must be registered in a national database, and smart owners will be sure their contact info is kept up-to-date. Additionally, not every shelter or veterinary clinic has a scanner, nor do most folks who might pick up and try to return a lost pet.

Best bet: Get both!

> **Did You Know?**
>
> **Some communities have created regular dog runs and separate spaces for small dogs.** These small dog runs are ideal for introducing puppies to the dog park experience. The runs are smaller, the participants are smaller, and their owners are often more vigilant because they are used to watching out for their fragile companions